The

TINCTURE

of

TIME

. . .

A Memoir of (Medical) Uncertainty

ELIZABETH L. SILVER

PENGUIN PRESS

New York

2017

PENGUIN PRESS
An imprint of Penguin Random House LLC
375 Hudson Street
New York, New York 10014
penguin.com

Library of Congress Cataloging-in-Publication Data

Names: Silver, Elizabeth L., 1978– author.
Title: The Tincture of Time: A Memoir of (Medical)
Uncertainty / Elizabeth L. Silver.
Description: New York: Penguin Press, 2017.
Identifiers: LCCN 2016043492 (print) | LCCN 2016058648 (ebook) |
ISBN 9781101981443 (hardcover) | ISBN 9781101981467 (e-book)
Subjects: LCSH: Infants—Diseases. | Parenthood. |
BISAC: BIOGRAPHY & AUTOBIOGRAPHY / Personal Memoirs. |
BIOGRAPHY & AUTOBIOGRAPHY / Medical. | FAMILY &
RELATIONSHIPS / Parenting / General.
Classification: LCC RJ45 .S545 2017 (print) |
LCC RJ45 (ebook) | DDC 618.92—dc23
LC record available at https://lccn.loc.gov/2016043492

Printed in the United States of America
1   3   5   7   9   10   8   6   4   2

Designed by Amanda Dewey

For A

Doubt is not a pleasant condition,
but certainty is an absurd one.

—*Voltaire*

Author's Note

This book is an amalgamation of how I coped with the hospitalization and rehabilitation of my infant child. It is the abstract
world of unknown health that captured my attention outside the
personal narrative, and because of that, this book is not just my
story, but the story of others, too. Because of this, I have changed
the names of many people with whom I have spoken, to protect
their privacy, with the exception of some experts. Though I am
not a psychologist, psychiatrist, or physician, I have cited many of
them in the book, and their collective education has helped me
understand several medical and philosophical theories at once
confounding and satisfying. My investigation into medical uncertainty extends far beyond this book. I learned of cases of medical uncertainty as fleeting as a skinned knee or a twenty-four-hour
inability to breastfeed and as extended and permanent as a cancer

diagnosis or inherited neurological degenerative disease. Nevertheless, it bears noting that this book is not a psychological study, but rather my own exploration of what it means to cope with medical uncertainty as a patient, as a parent, and as a writer. Many kind individuals, friends and otherwise, have also consciously chosen to disclose their stories to me, and I am well aware that people who chose to do so may be fairly well along in terms of acceptance and awareness of their current medical states.

Most important, my devotion remains with my family, who have suffered enough merely by sharing blood with or marriage to a writer. This is my narrative, not theirs. They are the arbiters of their own stories, and since those perspectives belong to them, it will be their choice if, when, and what to share. It is for this reason that I have also changed the name of my daughter.

Part One

ACUTE

UNCERTAINTY

. . .

Acute

1. Referring to a health effect, brief; not chronic;
sometimes loosely used to mean severe.

2. Referring to exposure, brief, intense, short-
term; sometimes specifically referring to brief
exposure of high intensity.

—*Stedman's Medical Dictionary*

I WAS TEN YEARS OLD when I watched my first surgery.

It was an emergency appendectomy that turned out to be cancer of the appendix, and in hindsight, the procedure has grown to become an indelible marking of my childhood. A turning point, an experience earned like a divot on the wooden panel of my youth, watching a live operation was like growing an extra inch and marking it with a fat line. I think back to that night when, as a child, I watched another person befall the scalpel and willingly allow the body to unbolt. My adult eyes reimagine organs, multicolored and sealed with a mucous lining of blood, cleared for the taking, for rearranging, for tinkering; but at the time, it was probably just various shades of red.

My father and I were at home alone. It was 1989 and summer in New Orleans. Expats in the Bayou town, my family tasted the fried sweetness of beignets whenever guests visited, and shouted,

"Throw me something, mister," a Mardi Gras catchphrase, as frequently as "Are we there yet?" on one of our long car drives out of New Orleans to visit family in New York or California. The weather was humid, and thick, moist air traveled heavy into our daily lives, making it difficult to do just about anything. New Orleans was built below sea level, though I didn't understand what that meant until I moved away at thirteen and learned that people in other places were ordinarily buried below ground. Exquisite aboveground tombs were the norm, jambalaya was on every menu, and Mardi Gras was a week off from school. New Orleans, a rare tourist haven for Americans to visit and feel as though they'd traveled abroad, was our hometown of narrative excess. Jazz, crime, historic architecture, culinary delight, and my family all mingled together.

For half of my childhood, our little family unit lived in Louisiana without a strong connection to the area, aside from the medical position that brought my father there. My parents had left their own parents, siblings, and friends behind in Los Angeles, where they had met and married. In New Orleans, we lived in a suburb on the West Bank of the Mississippi River in Algiers Parish. My father (an infant Holocaust survivor who was raised in Poland, Germany, and Baltimore) and my mother (born and raised in Brooklyn until she transplanted to Los Angeles with her family in the 1960s) settled in the Bayou suburbs to raise their three young children. Pregnant in the late 1970s with me, her third, my then urban-centric mother chose to drive an extra thirty minutes to give birth at a hospital inside the city limits purely so that the words "New Orleans" and not an unknown suburb would be written on my birth certificate. New Orleans, despite its welcome streets and pleasant reputation, was not my parents' home, either. So without family to help, when the emergency call for an appendectomy came in the middle of the night, my father had no choice but to bring me with him.

He was in his surgical prime, the treasured midforties, and had been paged to the hospital for a routine operation. I don't remember where I was sleeping or what I was wearing, but I do recall my father waking me up in the middle of the night telling me we had to go. Now.

"It's just an appendectomy," he said as I rubbed my tired eyes. "Shouldn't take longer than half an hour."

I nodded. My older sister was away at camp, and my mother was driving my older brother through a pop-up map of small towns in the South for sport competitions. My father was on call as a general surgeon. HIPAA, the Health Insurance Portability and Accountability Act, would not yet be enacted for another seven years, and anonymity in medicine was as present as, well, child voyeurs in operating rooms. At the time, no one seemed particularly concerned about his taking me inside. In fact, my father told me years later that he had wanted me to observe so that I could share the experience with him. He did the same for my sister, who eventually became a doctor herself.

Because it was late in the evening, there wasn't anyone to sit with me in a waiting room, so the nurses scrubbed me in, fussing over me with juvenile exhilaration as people fuss over dolls. I was small, freckled, and brunette, a bit chubby around the knees, and dressed in oversized blue scrubs marked with an XS and stamped with the name of the hospital on the top and bottom. Mammoth sinks, great canyons of sterling silver, lined the walls. Someone scooped me up and leaned me over a sink to help me wash my hands. I remember learning the word "sterilization" that night.

My father stepped on a pedal beneath the sinks, and water appeared as if out of a fountain. A nurse then picked up two rubber gloves and opened them wide, directing my father's small hands to slip into the powdery rubber, covering not only his hands but also the sleeves of his surgical gown, so that no skin was exposed. He was ready. He motioned to a nurse, who pulled down his surgical mask so I could see his face. By his expression, his silent words, I knew to pay attention.

"Stand right here," someone told me once we'd entered the operating room, and I did, as if I had been put in a time-out and forced to stand in one place for hours as punishment. In reality, though, it was the opposite in every way that matters. I said nothing while I watched life transform from several feet away. I wasn't observing from above in a surgical theater, nor was I a terrified loved one on the other side of the solid door. I was standing in the corner, shivering from the air-conditioning and trying to count the goosebumps as they rose from my skin. I was standing in the corner, smelling the iodine and alcohol-cleansed instruments. I was standing in the corner, on the inside.

Time has a way of stretching details to fit our present needs, but there are a few particulars that have remained as powerful today as they were twenty-five years ago. First, the stark color contrasts that accompanied the initial incision. The patient's abdomen (though I can't remember if it belonged to a man or a woman) was pale white against the iodine: a thick yellow was brushed over the skin to prevent infection, and the patient's body no longer seemed human, but rather like a workbench.

Words were exchanged, and then almost out of nowhere, a line of dark crimson appeared. Centimeters, maybe; a foot long perhaps—I can't recall. This was before laparoscopy and the preservation of bikini lines, so surgeons were able to cut wherever best for the surgery itself. I don't even remember seeing the scalpel cut into flesh when the dark line appeared. The patient (was it a man or a woman?) was lying behind a curtain of blue paper, asleep, with her (or his?) belly intact, until the blood appeared. It's this palette that I haven't forgotten. Creamy white, bright yellow, and then the dark line of red. A sort of medical color primer for beginners.

My father and the others were talking, I know. I heard them, but I don't recall a single word. I was fixated, trying to watch, hoping to see what I could from my little corner on the inside.

Once the incision was made, hands (presumably my father's) opened the body and flipped the skin to the sides, like pages of a book. Years later, I realized that what I saw beneath the skin that day was an exceptional story, perhaps the most exceptional of my life. A profound origin parable for all. Inside this body—*all* bodies—was a basket of objects making life.

The second memory homes in on a dissonant sense of sound.

Dark blood continued to fill the open body, making it difficult for the surgeons to navigate the organs and even more difficult to remove what wasn't working. A nurse following my father's orders used a long plastic tube to remove excess blood so that he could more clearly see the internal organs. Like the suctioning of saliva at the dentist, the suck-suck-suck of internal fluids traveling from a body to a bag through this plumbing device was all I could hear for the rest of the operation. It was the only part of the three-hour surgery that left me queasy.

After that, everything in my memory goes blank. A fast-forwarding of life, blackened by dim lights and dark colors. Twenty-five years later, my father and I both remember that evening with fondness. I suspect this shared moment of intimacy had as much impact on him as it did on me, because no matter how or when it comes up, his response is always the same:

"Lizzy, remember that time you came and watched me do surgery? It was supposed to be a little appendectomy, thirty minutes at most, and it turned out to be cancer of the appendix! You saw a good one."

"I do!" I exclaim each time it comes up, which is more frequently than may seem healthy. We both get equally excited, particularly because the patient's cancer was discovered and removed so early.

At ten, I had been reading *Anne of Green Gables*, learning fractions and decimals, and wanting to have sleepovers with my friends. Admittedly, I had been privileged. I'd seen little of violence or trauma in my young life, yet the crisp redness of blood hardly bothered me. In many ways, perhaps, it even fueled me to understand where it came from, what it did.

To some, this excess thrill may sound callous. To others, the joy surgeons take in a successful and life-affirming choice of work is obvious. They view a problem and are trained to go in and fix it, just like a repairman, which is why they are often nicknamed the mechanics of the medical world. Our excitement stemmed from my father's having facilitated a clear solution to someone's health problems. Removing that emotional bond empowers and enables these trained technicians to perform their highly skilled jobs effectively. So each time my father's face lit with enthusiasm remembering the appendectomy, he was reliving that sense of challenge and accomplishment. At ten, this made perfect sense to me. When there is a problem, cut it out and allow the body to heal.

That evening spent with my father quickly became the guiding thread of my own medical story: that of a person who refused to find fear in an operating room or hospital, who trusted medicine and those who practice it faithfully, who believed an answer existed where a doctorate resided, who silently judged those who questioned the clarity of science, who refused to worry about the answers, because they would come. They always did. Certainty in medicine, like the New York subway system, always seemed to arrive, even if occasionally a few minutes late. The answers were comforting, available, and effortlessly clear, until they were not.

A Two-Headed Beast

Like most writers, I have unpublished work sitting on my hard drive. My twenties were spent working in writing-related jobs, traveling, teaching English, and in graduate school for both creative writing and law. I wrote two novels before selling my third, which appeared in bookstores one week after I learned I was pregnant. I spent three years in law school and another two as a judicial clerk, apprenticing for a judge in Texas, learning an entirely different way to write, all while continuing to write fiction at night, during my lunch breaks, and in the early hours before donning my suit and heels and driving to court. But my first two books, the ones that I call my stillborn novels, both begin in emergency rooms. It's not that I planned this kinship. Like my own life, the lives of these books begin in the heightened drama of a hospital.

Perhaps there is something romantic about the intensity of emergency rooms that attracts me to the subject matter. Great orbits of mystery, misery, hope. Platforms for dramatic storytelling. Emergency rooms are spaces filled with anticipation, primal in their emotional pull. Broad cross-sections of society—perhaps more accurate than jury duty in reflecting a community—they present humanity at its most raw. Illness escapes no one and injury has no favorites. Good health is an unrigged lottery. Despite some people's attempts at warding away illness and injury and even death, at some point in time, at least one comes for everyone.

In Greek mythology, there is a well-known gatekeeper to the underworld, Cerberus, a polyheaded beast who resides as a face of fear for so many heroes trying to pass through to the other side. In paintings and in literature, he can take shape with as few as two, or as many as fifty, heads, though most representations depict him with three. A canine monster who glances in all directions; his gaze cannot be escaped. Whether quadrupled or multiplied by the dozens, the eyes of Cerberus monitor the entrance and exit of the underworld, allowing some in and others out.

Emergency room triage, the process by which medical experts decide who is seen first based on urgent medical need, is not unlike this mythological beast, guiding some souls in and refusing entry for others. Though it is a Hospital to all, it can represent either Hades or Heaven, depending on your perspective. Some souls will remain forever in the underworld of hospitals, while others are lucky enough to escape.

On March 12, the day my husband, Amir, and I learned that our six-week-old daughter fell victim to seizure, we came face-to-face with this two-headed beast twice—once in the afternoon and once in the late evening in an entirely different hospital.

Children's Hospital

It's around nine o'clock in the evening, the dawn of springtime in Los Angeles. Our daughter, Abby, was born just six weeks earlier in the height of winter, and Amir and I had left the hospital in

T-shirts and flip-flops, laughing, chatting, speaking to everyone in our line of vision about our new daughter. On this evening in March, though, we drive to Children's Hospital Los Angeles in muted silence. Something is wrong but we don't speak about it. Instead, I sit in the back beside Abby's car seat while Amir drives the few miles across town.

We park and walk into the emergency department with a conflicted sense of urgency and composure. One hand grips my phone and another my driver's license and insurance card, while Amir cradles Abby in his arms. Abby appears healthy. No scrapes coat her face; no bruises, cuts, or other stains of a fall adorn any part of her complexion. We had unknowingly dressed her in the same outfit she had worn home from the hospital forty-four days earlier when she was still acquainting herself with the world. A striped overnight Onesie with attached feet and a bunny rabbit on the front. Amir and I had both agreed when we purchased it that it would do: it wasn't too girly, had no silly phrases on it like "Princess" or "Daddy's Little Girl" or "Mommy's Sweetie." Although we wanted to avoid genderizing colors altogether, the soft ears of the bunny, long and bursting with pink fleece comfort, sold us. This would be her hospital outfit.

A little boy, perhaps seven or eight years of age, waits with his father on the line at the intake desk just before us. I had seen them walking in while we were parking. The little boy doesn't look sick, either.

"It's a three-hour wait," the intake nurse tells the father, as he tries to express the severity of his son's condition. I can see it in the father's face. Wrinkles sprouting. Puffs of short breath. Panic. *What will become of my son? When can we see a doctor? We need a doctor now,* he must be thinking.

Amir kisses Abby's forehead and bounces her lightly on his chest while he finishes speaking. I want him to speak faster.

"Shhhhh," Amir whispers into her ear. "Shhhhhhhh."

As soon as the father finishes filling out his paperwork, I watch them journey to find an open seat relatively distant from coughing adolescents and crying toddlers, while we are called by the intake nurse.

I lean over to kiss Abby on her cheek. It is still and quiet.

Amir, a physician himself who refuses to introduce himself as a doctor or use his professional medical identity for favors, steps forward and speaks first, succumbing to parental necessity.

"Our six-week-old has been vomiting for twenty-four hours," he tells the intake nurse, calmly, as if rounding on any patient.

"She was born healthy, full term via cesarean six weeks ago. But in the last few hours, she has been experiencing what we think are seizures. A neonatologist friend saw a video we took of her and told us to go straight to the emergency room. So here we are."

My phone is ready, and as soon as the nurse asks, I press play on the first of four videos that would be replayed dozens of times over the next few weeks.

"OK," she says eventually, scrutinizing the screen halfway through the first video. "I see what you're talking about. That *could* be something." She points for Amir to wait with Abby by the entrance to the gate while I finish the registration. She tells us we'll be seen next.

Amir rushes to the corner of the room just beside the entrance to the department, covering Abby to protect her from airborne illnesses floating around the ER waiting room, and I complete the paperwork. Within minutes, Abby is in triage, held by another nurse taking her vitals, when her right arm begins to twitch like a torn electrical wire.

"See," we say, directing her attention back to Abby. "Now it's getting worse."

Her arm twitches in syncopation with the corner of her mouth, while the time between the movements grows shorter and the movements themselves larger.

"Look!" I say. "Is it a seizure? It looks like a seizure."

I glance at Amir who refuses to abandon Abby's gaze.

I ask again.

"Is it a seizure?"

It isn't a full-body seizure—that, I know. It isn't grand mal, the type that involves both the loss of consciousness and full-bodied muscle contractions. I replay the conversation over the phone when we sent the videos to friends-in-the-know.

It looks like it could be a focal seizure. If it were my kid, I'd go to Children's Hospital right now.

I am comforted when doctors say things like this. *If it were me, I'd do this. If it were my kid, I'd go here.* It lends a sense of intimacy, shared experience, family. We are all in this together.

"Is it a seizure?" I ask again. Nobody answers.

"Let's go," the triage nurse says in a conflicting balance of calmness and urgency. She carries Abby away, leading us from triage through the narrow hallways and into the intestines of the emergency department. All around us are rooms in which infants and toddlers, adolescents and young adults, are subjects on examining tables. In each room, teams of professional arms stretch outward from nameless patients, whose faces are etched in anguish. There are cries and calm voices, orders barked and orders melodically requested. People speaking in English, in Spanish, in Mandarin, in Japanese, in Russian, all operating as part of the machinery of the department. Each person has a role to play and, color coded by scrubs, fulfills it.

We follow the nurse holding Abby until we come to a private room, and she hands Abby to someone else. I don't know anyone's name. I don't know anyone's education or training or years of experience, save a snap judgment I often make on age. At least a dozen medical providers swarm over her, pushing Amir and me to the edges, where the macabre beauty of science materializes in seconds. A perverse tableau plucked from the cutting-room floor of a B-rated horror film blocks before us frame by frame.

Frame One: Nurses and physicians and assistants hold down her nine-pound body on the gurney. At least eight wires are attached to her torso, a nasal cannula taped around her cheeks. Round silver stickers suction to her chest to account for her pulse, her breathing, her heart rate.

Frame Two: She is crying, her tears and hysteria escalating as they insert an IV catheter into the only hair-sized vein they can tap. Access through both feet and one hand has been blown from an earlier ER visit. This is not our first visit of the day. This was not the first time something seemed wrong. The firsts don't always seem so frightful when they appear. Outliers, accidents, but not reality. Twice, of course, is a concern; three times, a pattern. We didn't want to wait for a pattern to emerge.

Frame Three: Wires snake through her, a Luis Buñuel film come to life. Hands levitate around her, eventually holding down her arms and legs. They are blue, covered by plastic to protect everyone, except for me. Someone wearing blue scrubs tells us we can come to her side and comfort her, so my naked hand is now on top of her, too, holding a light blue pacifier in her mouth.

Frame Four: An IV is connected to the catheter in her hand. Phenobarbital is administered through the IV to stop the seizures. White ID bracelets tag her left ankle while a splint is taped around her arm to keep the IV in place.

Frames Five through Eight: Needle upon needle is removed from plastic casings and inserted into her foot and into the back of her hand for fluids, for administration of future medication, for conscious sedation, for blood cultures—all to find the etiology of the seizure, its origin. And to stop it.

Frame Nine: Something goes wrong. A needle inserted outside a vein, a tearing of the skin, a spilling of blood.

"Liz!" I hear, and then look down.

Blood is dripping all over my hands and clothes as if I'm

awakening to a crime I accidentally committed. *These are not my hands. This is not my blood,* I think, with more fear than if it had been. *This is not my blood. This is not my blood. This is not my blood,* I keep saying to myself as if I can stop the worst from transpiring, whatever that is.

"Don't worry," I hear, as someone else wipes my hands with water and gauze and soap and a tenderness that feels misplaced.

"It's just your daughter's blood," I hear.

"From the needle sticks," I hear again.

I look around.

"It's Abby's blood," Amir says, when I look to my hands in confused terror.

Frame Ten: I look back to the gurney. The medication begins to take effect, and Abby is no longer seizing. She is no longer writhing on the oversized pediatric gurney. Instead, it seems like she is calmly listening to the doctors call out tests to perform and procedures to attempt.

Let's get anaerobic and aerobic blood cultures times two. Let's get a CBC with diff. Sed rate. Glucose.

Words spill at a rapid pace, if they are even those words. I'm sure there are more. More words and treatments that will never be captured in the frames of my memory. I grab Amir's hand, and in my mind, search for the corner in the old Bayou operating room, as if my father could look over to me, pull down his mask, and smile.

Wow, that was exciting, wasn't it, Lizzy? Newborn seizures, and we stopped them!

Abby is now still. Eyes as immobile as her body. A soul locked in.

The first of many procedures is now complete. Next comes the scan that tells a new story altogether.

IT IS JUST BEFORE MIDNIGHT. Plastered across a computer screen on the hallway wall is the topography of Abby's brain in black-and-white. At six weeks, her skull is not fully hardened, its plates just barely connecting at the top to form a thick white shell. Fuzzy grey matter, like snow on an old 1950s television, occupies most of what lives inside the white shell, but in the center there is a massive shape, geometrically confused. A white circle with a white arrow climbing out from underneath, like the root of a tooth. The root on the other side of the circle is black, representing normal brain ventricles filled with cerebrospinal fluid.

I know that white indicates blood on a CT scan, while black could be a mass. Knowledge that it could be a tumor or a cyst, for example, is the product of a life peripheral to medicine and a handful of visits to ERs for minor injuries.

"It's not good," the ER physician says to us.

Her voice is blunted with sentiment, as though she's using a metal hammer tipped with padding.

"I'm so sorry," she continues. "It's a bleed."

In Abby's scan, so much is white. If her brain were an egg, the entire yolk would have been compromised.

The Gatekeeper

In those frozen moments following the discovery of the bleed but before transport to the neonatal intensive critical care unit (NICCU) upstairs, Amir and I sit in a new ER examining room, awaiting a bed for Abby. We don't look at each other. Our mutual silence blares. No moments of embrace, no initiation of discussion of what we had just seen on the computer screen. Just motionless stares at the wall, where a cartoon dictating pain thresholds from one to ten hangs by a loose wedge of Scotch tape.

Fluorescent lights fill the sounds until the intake nurse walks into the room.

"I just wanted to let you know that how you came into the ER changed everything for me," she tells us.

Hours earlier, we had entered the ER like every other patient or parent with the drugged-out face of fear. We walked in as calmly as possible, played her the videos, gave her the summary of events, and awaited entry to the magical fortress behind the gate, the same one I believed would fix Abby and send us home. But she tracked us down. She remembered what was said, or what was not said. She remembered the evidence captured in our hands.

"You showed me that video and because of that, I pushed you to the front of the line," she says to us. "That decision saved your baby's life."

While this may or may not be true and is likely enhanced by self-aggrandizement, I feel, for a split second, simultaneously relieved and guilty, as if her choices (or even mine) pushed me ahead of other deserving patients, as if being seen so quickly was actually warranted. Nothing happening seems warranted.

Instead, the intake nurse became Cerberus, taking down notes for each person who entered, determining who would get to go behind the gate. *Cerberus*, with its etymology burned into our present reality. *Cer*berus, *cere*brum, *cere*bellum—a return to the multiheaded beast of mythological fame. Clearly, what she wanted to say was: It was *my* actions that helped. *I* saved your daughter's life.

There is something about certainty, in and out of medicine, that drives people to point the arrow inward. We want to believe that we are responsible for positive outcomes and concrete results. If we are in any way connected to an incident, we must know its outcome. This isn't necessarily narcissism, but rather a human need to feel connected to others' triumphs or tragedies. It is the necessary and inevitable integration of lives that causes this. *Might I have had a part in helping? In hurting?* Our roles are all individual tracks in a collective transport.

This woman wasn't able to leave work that night and drive home without knowing for sure what had happened to the seizing infant. Was it the commonly seen infant seizures of unknown origin? More perilous infantile spasms? A reflection of something else? She needed some form of certainty. She needed to know.

ER One

Two nights before the seizures began, Abby vomited in large pools all over Amir. Well-earned, savagely pumped milk curdled on his clothing and in clumps over the couch, and seeped into the pores on our rug. We calmed her; we cleaned her; we looked to one another, relatively calm. Having seen far worse during his training, Amir was scarcely bothered by the vomit. A childhood of my father shrugging off such staples of life in relatively minor symptoms inoculated me, too, from grave concern. Children get sick. They vomit. Sometimes they have fevers.

That same day at three in the morning, while I was nursing her, it happened again. I woke Amir and though we comforted her, still we both realized that this was on the checklist of parenthood. Clean up vomit. Change diaper. Serve Pedialyte. Kiss and embrace your baby. She easily fell asleep in my arms, beloved and calm.

But early the following morning when she vomited a third time, I called her pediatrician, and the on-call doctor instructed me to give her Pedialyte for the day and keep a close watch. "She may need to go to the ER for IV fluids," the doctor said to me over the phone. The possibility of an IV removed me from complacence for the first time, and so I opened my computer and began googling "emesis," the medical term for vomiting, in newborns. Unbeknownst to me, Amir and my father were doing the same.

We all came to the same conclusion: this looked a lot like

pyloric stenosis, the narrowing of the pylorus, which is the opening from the stomach into the small intestine. Although more complicated than an appendectomy, particularly on a newborn, the solution for this problem would be relatively simple: a surgical procedure to unblock the pylorus to allow contents to flow from the stomach to the intestines. It's a procedure my father had performed a hundred times. It would be nerve-racking and invasive, but straightforward, something that could be fixed.

My brother, Sasha, and I took Abby to the doctor the following morning with this diagnosis in mind. Abby was no longer vomiting. The pediatrician, a skilled, kind, young physician, took time to humor my research and agreed that Abby might be suffering from pyloric stenosis. She sent us to the emergency room for an ultrasound to either confirm or rule it out, and for Abby to receive IV fluids for possible dehydration. Her office wasn't equipped with the technology, which was the only reason to visit the hospital.

Within moments of arrival, I was placed on the gurney as the patient with Abby on my lap, apparently standard procedure in an adult hospital. Eventually two nurses pricked Abby with the care of a blind couple attempting needlepoint.

"Can you get a NICCU nurse to do this?" I asked, as Abby's screams punctured the door of the room.

"There aren't any available," they said. "It could be hours and we need to get the IV in."

"I know," I said, turning away. "Just do it then. She needs the fluids. Just get the IV in."

Three of her limbs were used and tightened with a tourniquet to find a proper vein, and none of the attempts was successful. The discarding of an arm, an elbow fold, a cushioned foot bulbous with baby fat.

I turned back to Abby and wiped her tears.

Drops of blood collected at the hole in her wrist where they were unable to properly insert an IV, and so they squeezed some of it into a vial.

"I'm so sorry," they said. "But we can at least get some blood this way for the lab."

We were wheeled out of the emergency room to imaging, where Abby was prepped for the abdominal ultrasound. The room was small, the lights dim. The main source of light was from the various green, red, and white bulbs and cursors blinking from the computers on the walls and probes on nearly every edge of space.

The technician, a middle-aged man with a bushy mop of gray and brown hair, tried to make her smile as he spread ultrasound gel across her belly.

"It's warm," he said. "I don't want her to be any more uncomfortable than she already is."

I smiled, nodding *thank you*, and held her close to my chest, nursing her throughout the short procedure, the best way to ensure stillness and accuracy. It was in that dark room with Abby's shit-filled diaper pressed against my legs that I first noticed it. Little twitches to her right hand that looked vaguely suspicious.

After one or two times, I glanced at the ultrasound technician.

"Did you notice that?"

"No," he said. He was focusing on the screen before him, shifting and placing the ultrasound probe on Abby's tiny belly, attempting to take as many photos of its interior in the rare moments she was still.

"Shhhh," I whispered in Abby's ear, trying to calm her so that the technician could complete his job. "It's going to be OK. Shhhhh."

Instead of watching the monitor, I stared at Abby's arm to see if it moved again. Was she going to jerk in that barely-there rhythm that might have occurred? Or might not have? Maybe it's just newborn fidgeting. Or maybe she was just uncomfortable from the warm gel on her belly.

When it happened again, it was a movement so slight and hidden that, unless observed closely, it would likely go unnoticed. The radiology tech announced the end of the test.

AS THE NURSES WHEELED US back to our room in the ER, the attending physician called out to me.

"She looks good. Blood tests came back. She's not dehydrated. No pyloric stenosis. You can take her home!"

I never saw him again. I can't even remember what he looks like. If he was old, young, bald, short, wearing scrubs or a white coat. He was a man—that I remember, and nothing else. But it didn't matter because Abby would not need abdominal surgery. She would not need to be hospitalized beyond this emergency room. Nor was she dehydrated. All of those attempts to insert the IV were for naught, her six-week-old limbs serving as practice cushions for the nurses. A small price to pay to be able to leave the hospital healthy.

My brother, Abby, and I waited a bit longer for discharge. We called Amir, my parents, my in-laws, and were ready to leave when the pediatric resident finally visited our room.

He asked me if I noticed anything different in her behavior, apart from the vomiting.

After a grateful sigh of relief, I almost said nothing.

"Yes," I eventually told him, describing the arm movements— slight, nearly undetectable, infrequent.

The resident briefly examined Abby, but she was not doing anything out of the ordinary. Her hands were still, her arms cradled in mine, her eyes closed. She was resting, waiting for discharge.

"Just keep an eye on it and put your hand over her hand if it happens again," he said. "If you can't stop the movements, then it may be a seizure. But she's looking good now."

And that was that. We were discharged.

When my brother and I returned home an hour later, Amir was eagerly awaiting us.

"Good news," I told him. "She doesn't have pyloric stenosis. Also, she's not dehydrated, but I noticed this weird arm movement. Just keep an eye on it and tell me if you see it."

I hopped in the shower. When I finished, he told me he saw it, too. We both focused on it with a watchful eye. We ordered dinner—Chinese food from our favorite delivery—relaxed, and played with Abby.

It happened again.

"There it is," I said.

Amir nodded.

"Let's record this," we both said.

It was just after six p.m.

An Entrance and an Exit

Tom Stoppard writes in the play *Rosencrantz and Guildenstern Are Dead* that his players should "look on every exit as being an entrance somewhere else." A singular reality set against multiples, a jarring juxtaposition in full. For example, the exit from an emergency department is often an entrance back to a car, the streets, the home; or it veers toward a hospital bed, or even the outcome least desirable. Our exit from the emergency department at Children's Hospital to the entrance of intensive care is a path that feels complete, expected. Once Amir, Abby, and I enter the next phase, we assume we'll have more answers.

Upon admission to the unit, we trail behind hospital personnel until arriving at our destination: a hospital room, adorned with a wall full of outlets for dozens of machines if they become necessary, a sink, a computer, and a curtain. The centerpiece of this outrageously priced bedroom is not a bed or a crib, but a plastic box, an incubator that magnifies the rest of the room in contrast. I've been in dozens of hospital rooms but was used to seeing the gurney, the wheeled bed with white sheets and a blue blanket taking over the square footage of space. Here space is reserved for the medical personnel swimming in and out of their habitat, a moat protecting the castle of plastic at the center. Nurses and medical assistants shift Abby from the gurney to the incubator, an invisible fence from which we are promptly cut off.

I watch from a distance as she is transferred and settled, as plans are made to begin an extraordinary workup. I know it shouldn't be me, but I can't help but want it to be me who carries Abby through this transition, calming her, kissing her, telling her she's going to be fine, even if it could be an explicit lie. Nor is it Amir, whose massive six-foot-three frame dwarfs her twenty-two inches by mere proximity. Instead, expectedly, a nurse cradles her body, spotted red with pinpoint scabs from excess needle draws, taking over our roles.

"There, there, princess," she says. "There, there."

My mouth drools with unformed sentences. From a distance, I watch as this woman tends to my daughter. From the sidelines, I can only smell my daughter, hear my daughter, do anything but touch my daughter. Where my hand would otherwise have cradled her infant fingers is a white splint, taped around her fidgeting limbs to keep the IV intact. A thick wire tunnels through her outer palm while plastic seals it in, pulling her skin so tight that her hand ages instantly, its wrinkles prominently captured under the translucent tape. Wrapped around her big toe, just inches below, is a miniature pulse oximeter, radiating red light through all of her foot. At that moment, Abby's hands and feet beam, other-worldly.

"Oh, princess," the nurse says again, through a series of coos. "Look at all your hair. So, so beautiful."

Unlike most parents-to-be, from the moment I learned I was pregnant with a girl, I didn't fantasize about what she would look like, how she would sound, whether her personality would mimic mine or jump to the left hemisphere of the brain and resemble my husband's in its logic and scientific comprehension. No. Princesses were my concern, my main concern. I feared the possibility of a princess phase, unfairly quipping at distant family members who rejoiced in our pregnancy news by calling our unborn child "everyone's princess." I vowed to challenge any misogynistic statement that ushered my daughter into such a profoundly superficial world and instructed Amir to do the same.

"Sweet little princess," the nurse says again.

But I don't say a word. I don't want to upset the one person whose job it is to care for my daughter, whose responsibility it is to check her vitals hourly, make sure her temperature is normal, spot any seizure-like activity. So I say nothing, and there it is: the first of many plans for Abby suddenly gone quiet.

The nurse turns to us. "Perhaps you should get settled," she says.

She motions to the curtain behind us. I pull it back and find a mustard-yellow couch that would become our home for the fore-seeable future.

"Go wash your face, brush your teeth," she says.

I acquiesce. I have no will or reason to disagree. I find the bathroom. I splash water on my face and lean over the sink into the mirror. It's blurry. I'm blurry. My eyes tired, my skin broken out, new wrinkles pocketed on either side of my mouth. Water is dripping from my hands. The faucet is on, filling the basin with lukewarm foam. I look down and see it there from earlier in the evening—my daughter's blood splattered across my shirt.

Don't worry, I remember hearing when I saw blood on my hands hours earlier. *It's just your daughter's.*

Splashes of soap mix with it, a constellation of blood dotted across my chest, unprotected.

Days later, when my mother-in-law takes our clothing from the hospital to wash it for us, I forget to remove that shirt from the pile, and the blood is subsequently washed away. I'm furious with myself. If something even worse happens to Abby, I would want to hold on to it.

I look in the mirror again, my vision even more blurry and worn. My fingers are dry. I scratch my eyes, removing the old contact lenses. This is better, though. It's easier to see clearly when nothing else is in focus. I take off the shirt and tie it around my shoulders like a cape. At the moment, all I wish for is a prin-cess phase.

Malaysia

After driving our last visitor to the airport in early March, Amir, Abby, and I returned to our apartment, where for the first time since Abby's birth, we began to bind the familial tape around us as a newly formed unit. We cuddled in bed, surveyed the frozen foods in our freezer, stared at Abby, bathed Abby, compared our baby pictures to Abby, took turns awakening in the middle of the night for Abby, binged on Netflix television series, and generally ignored everyone on the outside for the first time since she was born. The delicacies of new parenthood at once unique and universal to almost every parent were finally served to us in the privacy of our own home. Then, on March 8, it was reported that a flight was missing somewhere over the Indian Ocean. Like the rest of the world, we were captivated, watching the twenty-four-hour news cycle from our familial cocoon.

Malaysia Airlines Flight 370 had vanished from air traffic control radar. A Boeing 777, the world's largest twinjet airliner, not only disappeared from a screen, but from the atmosphere, sky, and any reasonable tracking device. Twelve crew members and 227 passengers from fifteen countries were gone, liquefied, as if some sort of black magic eclipsed them.

Around-the-clock news stations took note, and for weeks this "Breaking Story," which carried with it almost no new breaking news at all, blasted "mystery" across the television and Internet, nourishing fear in those already ill with it.

Theories quickly floated around the circuitry of communication and conspiracy. Electronic hijacking; jihadi hijacking; a mass suicide; a phantom cellphone theory (which for several days assumed that everyone was alive on board but simply could not answer their phones, while the plane inconceivably hovered somewhere in the unknown atmosphere); a shooting-down of the plane over the deepest and most unreachable ocean on the globe (a bona fide Bermuda Triangle cornered in the depths of the Indian Ocean); consumption by a black hole (that had somehow reached the earth's outer layers from space); and, of course, an alien abduction. None of these theories was proved, and despite fifteen countries' financial support and incomparable manpower, the mourning families still have no answers. This investigation became the largest and most expensive search in history, and it produced no clarity. No crash site was found. No bodies floated to the surface of the water. It wasn't until sixteen months later that even a small piece of marine debris believed to be part of the plane was found in a remote area of the Indian Ocean, providing no real information of comfort to the families. Only theories of the realistic and fantastical variety.

At the height of this media maelstrom, Abby falls ill, at once distracting us from this international mystery and placing us in a much smaller one. Though her care involves no global cooperation or twenty-four-hour news cycles, hundreds of years of medical discoveries, intelligence, and practice come together as one in her first few days in the hospital.

NICCU

Once admitted into the NICCU from the emergency department shortly after midnight, we are taken on a tour of the unit, a massive floor with fifty-eight beds designed specifically for the care and attention of critically ill new life. As a Level I Pediatric Trauma Center, Children's Hospital Los Angeles receives not only babies admitted through their emergency department but also those from neighboring and distant hospitals. Almost every night, it seems, a helicopter lands above us, carrying with it a sick and premature newborn weighing less than a pound.

We are given parking passes and a set of sheets to soften the mustard-colored couch inside Abby's room. I am given plastic pumping parts so that I can continue to express milk for Abby on the hospital-grade breast pump should she need it once she's removed from her IV. After a quick glimpse into the pump rooms, I am shown how to label my product carefully so that it can be stored for future use. A perky social worker sits us down in the communal family room to await an orientation video.

"You are now in the newborn and infant critical care unit," someone says in the video. Amir and I haven't slept in more than twenty-four hours. A smear of hospital residue coats our skin. My eyes ache. I can feel the invisible contact lenses I've just removed shriveling from dryness against my line of vision. My hair is pulled back while Amir's is hidden under a baseball cap. No matter how helpful it is meant to be, the timing couldn't be worse for an orientation video. We had barely been oriented as parents outside the hospital, let alone inside its new parameters. I didn't remember where the bathrooms were, where the cafeteria was, when I'd be allowed visitors, or how to label my breast milk, let alone how to serve properly as a parent of a child, sick or healthy.

There is another father in the room also watching the video. A baseball cap covers the top half of his face, which, even through the shadows, I can see is raked with lines. We nod to him with closed-mouth smiles. He does the same in return. He tells us that he is awaiting the transport of his wife from another hospital, where she has been recovering from an emergency cesarean. Their child is born at twenty-something weeks, somewhere near the cutoff for viability, and he is completely alone. It is at this point I realize we are the lucky ones. We had been home with Abby for six weeks after an uneventful full-term delivery and hospital exit, tasting the comfort of normalcy, of nursing, of midnight feedings, of the awkward request for visitors to wash their hands upon entry. None of these parents was gifted even one night away from a hospital with their children before experiencing the same orientation. Amir and I don't have to explain that to each other. We know the minute we see this man biting his bottom lip, his eyes darting from side to side, his cuticles skinned around bloodied nail beds.

Moments later, the orientation video ends, and CNN returns to the airwaves. The Malaysian airplane is still missing.

MOST HOSPITALS around the country have neonatal intensive care units, or NICUs for short. They are not only care centers for ill babies, but also the site of new lives entering the world prematurely. These departments care for both the sick child and the family, inviting parents in as a means of comfort and support. In the Children's Hospital newborn and infant critical care unit (NICCU), Abby is the oldest kid on the block, the biggest baby in the ward. At times, she even appears the healthiest, as she was born full-term with all of her body parts properly formed. She stands out as the only baby on the floor with a full head of hair, sleeping among her ilk: a twenty-three-weeker, a preemie with cystic fibrosis, a baby born without a trachea.

At times, I have to walk out of the room to cry. At other points, I cower behind my sleeping curtain, my breasts raw from pumping. I check my email. I write to my editor: the paperback of my novel is scheduled to be published within weeks, and I am canceling events. I apologize. I apologize to them, to myself, to my literary career. I apologize profusely. I text. I email. I write. I read. I order books online. I carry a notepad with me everywhere I go to remember every detail, every blood splatter, every test, every question I have for myself, for Amir, for the medical team. When I wander the hallways, I peek into other rooms. I talk to other parents. I watch other parents. I scan the nursing staff. I long for intimacy and exercise and painkillers to numb the surgical scarring beneath my belly from the cesarean.

I roam the hallways, my hurried footsteps adding to the dissonant symphony of the NICCU. Mixed in with the beeps of monitors, the buzzing of pagers, and the frequent codes are the screams of ailing infants no longer sounding like babes. The cry of a sick infant quickly devolves into those of an animal. At home, this was the first sign that Abby was sick. Her cry changed. It lost volume, deflated in strength, and sounded like a cat's meow. I wasn't terribly concerned at the time. But in the NICCU, as her sound mixes with the other babies' and multiplies, it feels as though I'm walking through a pound full of ailing kittens. Occasionally, the scream of a tiger penetrates that sound, due most likely to a blood draw or re-insertion of an IV line, but mostly it is the cacophony of dozens of children aching to be heard.

Imaging

Twenty-four hours later, Abby needs more advanced imaging to properly map out the bleeding. Though the CT from the previous night in the emergency department had identified the bleed, it isn't able to comprehensively pinpoint its location. To find out specifically what parts of the brain are affected, how deeply, and whether or not the bleed extends beyond the ventricles and into the brain tissue, she needs an MRI.

This otherwise simple and noninvasive test is dangerous and potentially life threatening for infants. Though adults can undergo an MRI by merely lying down, squirmy newborns must endure anesthesia, made possible at this point by intubation, the perilous insertion of a tube into their small airways to facilitate breathing. Today intubation is a commonplace and simple procedure, but it was not always so, and is not without risk. In an infant, though, the airway into which the tube is inserted is so much smaller, more delicate, more easily torn without a full immune system to help repair any infection, and so this daily act in intensive care carries with it much more risk than on an adult.

As it is explained to us, though Abby has no trouble breathing, intubation and anesthesia is the best method of ensuring complete stillness to take reasonable and accurate images. Without anesthesia, Abby or any other infant would likely move, and with even slight movement, a repeat test would be required, delaying the investigation and the opportunity for more immediate intervention, if necessary.

We sign the paperwork. We agree to the intubation because we can't not.

The Tincture of Time

Time is inherently redefined in crises, and when lost within it, we forget its proper markers. When Abby is taken from us for imaging studies, we have time to think and talk for the first moments since rushing to the emergency department the day before. As we leave the hospital walls, heat and light engulf us. The MRI is an almost two-hour test that requires stillness from Abby and nothing of us but time. Time slowing down as if we are plucked into a surreal painting, our unknown futures dripping within Dalí's clock. Time freezing, as clusters of residents in blue and green scrubs laugh at an inside joke to my right. Time speeding up as their superiors rush to a food truck to my left, in rapid pace of food and consumption. The sun pierces. The breeze chills. The birds and bugs grow into monsters before my eyes. And again time slows down.

There was no separation between Abby and me six weeks ago. Six weeks. Fewer than fifty days. Nine months of carrying and eating. Nine months in which there was no distinction between mother and child. And now, only six weeks later, distance has not been fully established. Six weeks is a speck of time. Six weeks is just over a month. It's a hiccup in a lifetime, a splice of a pregnancy. Many women don't even know they are pregnant when they learn that they are six weeks along. My cesarean is still healing at six weeks. And now Abby is outside of my body and we are no longer one.

Amir and I sit in the courtyard of the hospital. I'm trying to grasp what it means to wait for the MRI to be finished, to find out if the bleeding has stopped or if it spread from the previous day.

"What happens if the bleeding gets worse?" I ask, knowing that it will probably mean neurosurgery. Maybe drilling a hole in her skull to release the blood and pressure. Maybe something worse.

"Let's wait and see," he says to me. He tells me months later that he knew there was a strong likelihood that Abby could have died. But now, all we can do is wait. *Let's wait and see* is all he can say.

"How long do you think it will be?" I ask. "Do you think it will take less than the two hours they told us?"

"I don't know," he says, his hands wrapped around a Styrofoam coffee cup. I know he doesn't want this role. He's neither neurosurgeon, neurologist, nor fortune-teller, but I ask him nonetheless, fully knowing that he has his own questions to ask, too.

"I don't think so," he says.

I look around at the trees and the blue sky.

"It's just a waiting game," he adds. "That's all. We have to wait."

"For the MRI results?"

"Uh huh."

"And then what? If the bleeding stops, then what?"

"It has to reabsorb. We won't be able to see what damage is there until the blood has reabsorbed. Then they'll do this again, take another picture of the brain without the blood there to see what remains."

"How long does that take?"

He shakes his head. He doesn't know.

"Days? Weeks? Months, maybe? There's a lot of blood in there."

"What if it doesn't reabsorb?" I ask.

Amir doesn't respond.

"We wait," I finally say, answering my own question. "We wait for it to reabsorb."

He drops his hand onto the table and I take it in mine.

"And if it doesn't?" I ask.

He stares at his coffee, unable to answer.

"Amir?"

"This is just the tincture of time," he says, looking back to me. "I sometimes write that at the bottom of my patient notes."

"What do you mean?" I ask.

"Sometimes there's nothing to do but allow time to be the potion, the medicine. Sometimes there is no medicine or treatment for a patient but time. Sometimes things get better on their own. So we sometimes say, 'It's the tincture of time.'"

He pauses, thinking aloud.

"People don't like to hear that."

News

I don't remember where I am or how I react when we learn that the bleeding is contained. As if borne from autonomic memory, it seems I always know. I don't remember sighing with relief or embracing Amir. I don't remember if I learn via her primary neonatologist or the radiologist, from the hospitalist or the nurse. What I do remember is that neither of us, Amir or me, is able to hold Abby. I remember that despite the controlled bleed, her condition is worsening. The intubation lasts longer than is anticipated and Abby develops respiratory complications from the procedure. She can no longer breathe on her own and is kept on a ventilator. I remember pumping breast milk at least six times a day and twice at night while at the hospital, and storing it all because she can't drink it.

But the bleeding has stopped. For now.

Next begins the investigation.

Testimony

It's a funny feeling to retell your story dozens of times a day. Each retelling becomes distorted. Based on the individual asking, you unconsciously choose to focus on one fact more than another, or subconsciously recall an incident differently based on your mood from hour to hour. This isn't necessarily by choice. It's human nature.

This is the central complaint with eyewitness testimony in criminal trials. Attorneys and juries rely on this seemingly innocuous form of evidence in so many ways to convict or exonerate defendants on trial for their freedom. A potential harm in the pathway to justice, this form of testimony is steeped in the subjective, the reflective, the human—an altogether necessary cognitive leap for relationships, but a thorny one for investigations of any form. After all, one person's memory will unknowingly evolve over time. Inherent biases, re-created memories, false histories, seep into stories without intent, and as a result, a crystallized narrative of a unified truth becomes impossible. Though documentation may frequently connect seamlessly to establish *the* overwhelming truth, variants inevitably find their ways in, making it nothing more than *a* truth.

The Innocence Project is an organization devoted to exonerating wrongfully convicted individuals of crimes for which they have been incarcerated. Citing century-old books as well as hundreds of verified scientific studies from recent decades, the organization often questions the reliability and usefulness of eyewitness testimony and identification while reviewing cases. Even in the early twentieth century, a book called *On the Witness Stand* was published in 1908, in which "the reliability of eyewitness identification" was called into question. This problem of eyewitness identification and memory is clearly anything but novel. In fact, a 1990 seventh circuit judicial opinion argued that "memory is highly suggestible—people are easily 'reminded' of events that never happened, and having been 'reminded' may thereafter hold the false recollection as tenaciously as they would a true one." The Innocence Project's Web site further states that "Yale Law professor Edwin Borchard found that eyewitness misidentification was the leading contributing factor of wrongful convictions in a 1932 book on the subject." This absurd phenomenon of relying on the unreliable was known nearly a century ago, but we return to it because, quite simply, there isn't a better option. We *need* that testimony, particularly when nothing else is available to help explain the truth.

The question then becomes, what is original memory? Is it a facsimile of what happened? A retelling? Is it a muted recounting of events, filtered through a perspective? It is impossible to re-create the precise language, the precise intonation, disposition, emotion behind a story when retold multiple times to multiple recipients. The listener is always different, and this inherently affects our ability to provide that universal story of truth. For an eyewitness providing evidence, this is crucial.

Eyewitness testimony and patient histories are close cousins with often similar fates. For a patient in a doctor's office, this narrative is equally significant in helping the doctor prescribe medications that will not contraindicate, or to help uncover a mystery illness. For parents trying to re-create a medical history or retell the events of what led to an illness that was not their own, the "eyewitness testimony" in this regard becomes as cloudy as if we are testifying to an event seen across the street in darkness during a sandstorm. We are all doing our very best with the facts we know in a language outside our own.

As I TELL ABBY'S MEDICAL HISTORY over and over again, on the phone, in ERs, to receptionists and triage nurses, ER attendants, and specialist after specialist, the events that bring us to them crystallize in my memory. Amir remembers the facts differently. (*She got* this *drug after Hematology visited,* he says. *No,* I remind him. *It was before.* We sit together and contemplate the order of events, and on and on it goes.)

The lawyer side of me hopes to be as complete and succinct as possible without any embellishment, while the novelist in me is desperate to provide a vivid narrative that I hope will help them solve the mystery. After all, something had to set off the bleed. We simply don't know what it is, and it is that mystery that causes the greatest concern. Without knowing why, how could they prevent recurrence? Without knowing why, how could they fix the source? And it is our narrative, our testimony, that will be key in beginning to formulate a plan to help her.

Starting Points

Amir and I settle back in the NICCU. Now that the bleed is stable, the medical team needs to find the source of it to properly treat, diagnose, and plan. They take over, hovering in and out of Abby's room, like ghosts whose presence is always felt, yet whose bodies are infrequently there for more than a minute. The typical origins of most bleeds do not fit with Abby's patient history, they tell us. Besides, right now, the process is all about stabilization and investigation. It is about finding the source, the origin, the culprit, the blame.

Bleeds, like all stories, have to start somewhere. A dot of food coloring dropped in a glass of water always starts as a single spot. But quickly, it marbles in the liquid, swimming in all directions and no direction in particular, with no specificity, no plan, no map for design. It spreads until you lose sight of the original drop. That source no longer exists.

Because nobody on Abby's initial medical team can determine the source of the bleed, we are like magnets, attracting almost every subspecialty that pediatrics has to offer. Neurology is called in. Then Hematology. General Pediatrics. Neurosurgery. Forensics. Ophthalmology. Radiology. Infectious Disease. Cardiology. Intensivists. Ear, Nose, and Throat. Abby is a self-contained enigma, despite a hefty team of specialists offering varied hypotheses. Each begins a workup of her case, all carrying a theory, a new set of tests, their respective training independent of the other. Sometimes they share their theories with one another. Sometimes not.

I learn how to summarize the events surrounding the seizures as succinctly as possible for both medical professionals and the social worker who has somehow worked her way into our hospital room. My perspective doesn't seem to matter, at least not yet. Nor do my opinions or emotions. Facts are all they need at this point, and they would all boil together in the cauldron of the differential.

A differential diagnosis is the systemic diagnostic tool used by physicians to weigh the possibility of one disease versus another based on symptoms. *Stedman's Medical Dictionary* defines it as "the determination of which two or more diseases with similar symptoms is the one from which the patient is suffering, by a systematic comparison and contrasting of the clinical findings." Linguistically, it is a singular plural: the finding of one diagnosis based on the possibility of many. In practice, it is a process of eliminating those many over testing and analysis to produce a singular finding. A differential diagnosis for something as simple as a cough may be a short or comprehensive list of all the possible conditions resulting from that one symptom. The omnipresent mobile phone app Diagnosaurus provides simple differentials for doctors. For example, *Cough, acute* reveals the following differential: (1) "viral upper respiratory infection"; (2) "bacterial upper respiratory infection"; (3) "postnasal drip"; (4) "pneumonia"; (5) "pulmonary edema from congestive heart failure"; (6) "pulmonary embolism"; (7) "GERD"; (8) "asthma"; (9) "side effect of drugs"; and so on. The doctor must then begin to eliminate some of those conditions by questions, by testing, and additional physical examination.

Once a diagnostic test (such as bloodwork, MRIs, CT scans, genetic mapping) is used, however, the differential may no longer be needed. It is only one factor that reflects the artistry and malleability of medicine. Creating a differential requires a comprehension of an aggregate, global picture that can come only with astute observation, and in many ways serves as the clearest example of why experience counts beyond test results and why surgeons (who are more technical) and internists (who are more diagnostic and interpretive) are often at odds. Medicine, as Dr. William Osler, one of the great fathers of the field, said to a class of graduating medical students in 1889, is an art:

> A distressing feature in the life which you are about to enter, a feature which will press hardly upon the finer spirits among you and ruffle their equanimity, is the uncertainty which pertains not alone to our science and art, but to the very hopes and fears which make us men. In seeking absolute truth we aim at the unattainable, and must be content with finding broken portions.

Indeed, art is a subjective field, and though medicine may find itself on similar subjective footing, it does so less willingly. It remains a mixture of science and art, objectivity and subjectivity, reactivity and proactivity. As patients, we assume medicine is objective science, and naturally we become frustrated when it is subjective, malleable, and often arrives in broken pieces. When Dr. Osler emphasizes the distress physicians are likely to experience, it is not due to the long hours or potentially squeamish scenes of injury, but rather the emotional organs of the practice. The lives of artists are often defined by their requisite malleability and subjectivity. They anticipate a specific and known lack of certainty in between their actions and successes. Moreover, their work often aims to expose these unknown truths of life. Yet "absolute truth," as Dr. Osler famously states, is something that is impossible to know—in and out of medicine—and accepting that, finding the "broken portions," is all part of the practice—for physicians and artists and laypeople alike.

ABBY'S TEAM BEGINS TO PROPOSE hypothetical answers, only to quickly dismiss them one by one, using new expert opinions and additional hypotheses.

She does not have a rare bleeding disorder, says Hematology after a handful of visits and a multitude of blood tests.

And she does not have an infection, rare or otherwise, bacterial or viral, says Infectious Disease.

And she has not experienced any trauma, never leaving our overly cautious sight.

And we have no genetic neurological disorders in our bloodline, at least none that we can track from both my husband's and my lineage, whose medical histories stretch back only a genera-

tion or two because three of our four sets of grandparents are
Holocaust survivors. Hitler eliminated our ability to trace long-
term medical history seventy years earlier. Plus, we'd both under-
gone genetic testing prior to Abby's conception, leaving us confident
in our reproductive gene pool.

She did have significant facial bruising upon delivery, but
that was presumably superficial and couldn't be connected to
head trauma so many weeks later. It was only a scapegoat and . . .
and . . .

and on we remain in the hospital, the subject of daily morning rounds with neurology, neurosurgery, hematology, infectious
disease, ophthalmology, neonatology, forensics, leading to complication upon complication without answers for the cause or resolution for the future. The unknown begetting more unknown.
Uncertainty surrounding us like a room full of mirrors, acute in
its urgency.

Social Workers

The patient histories taken by Abby's doctors go something
like this: Take me through what happened. Tell me about her
birth. Was there anything unusual about her delivery? Had she
been sick prior to this? Who had seen her? Had she been outside
of your care? What happened after the vomiting? How has her
eating been? Her latch? Tell me what happened at the first ER.
When did you first notice the seizures? How long were they? How

many did she have? How long did it last? Did you notice anything strange in her behavior leading up to this? Had she had seizures before? Has she had seizures since? Had you taken any antibiotics while pregnant? Had you had any surgeries while pregnant?

We reply with the same answers. The best answers we can provide. A testimony of slight variance from me to Amir and back again.

After twenty-four hours, though, we are visited by a social worker: a middle-aged woman, draped with a gold-plated *chai*, the Jewish symbol for life, around her neck. It seems unreasonably large. This is the same woman who took us on the three a.m. tour of the unit, who made us sit down and watch the orientation video's rules of NICCU cohabitation. This time, she walks in the room chipper and rehearsed, her overeager need to please as poorly disguised as the natural color of her hair.

"Think of me as your translator, your interpreter during your time here," she says. "If there is something you don't understand, if there is a medical term you didn't remember to ask the doctor," she says, "ask me."

I nod. Amir nods.

"If you need to speak with a doctor and one isn't here, just call me, and I'll see what I can do to get them back here to speak with you. OK?"

OK.

She then goes on to ask us the usual set of questions we'd previously heard.

"I hear you went to another ER earlier today. What happened there?"

I summarize the events. The pyloric stenosis. The dehydration. The abdominal ultrasound.

"When did you first notice the seizures?"

Earlier that day in the first ER.

"How many had she had?"

We're not one hundred percent sure. Maybe four episodes, but they got periodically longer, which is why we came here.

"Have you seen them before?"

Only today.

"What had she eaten?"

Only breast milk.

"Was she nursing normally?"

Yes, until two nights ago.

"How many times did she vomit?"

Four times.

"Did she have a fever?"

No.

"Did you give her Pedialyte?"

Yes.

"When did you call your pediatrician?"

The morning after the third emesis.

"Was she crying?"

On and off. But it sounded different. It was a different type of cry. Like an animal. A cat.

"Had she ever been out of your sight?"

No. Well, I mean, she had been with family shortly here and there, but no.

"Did you ever leave her unattended?"

No.

Of course not.

"Did you maybe ever just nod off and fall asleep, not knowing where she was? It's a common problem. Doesn't mean you did anything wrong."

No.

Wrong?

Nobody did anything wrong.

Why are you saying the word "wrong"?

"Have you ever just sat her on a table?"

The lawyer in me awakens in an instant. It is painfully clear what she is doing with her clipboard and questionnaire, her sense of outreach and protective seal. Do other people see through her movements, her actions, her scripted dialogue?

No, I say. Of course not.

"What about holding her?" she continues. "I know it's hard with new babies . . ."

Nobody actually falls for this.

Do they?

She looks to us as if she doesn't want to ask that question—the abuse question—but needs to. Amir and I don't have to speak to each other. It is the second time that day we communicate

without words or glances or body language. We both just know.
The social worker must, too. She moves on.

"Where does she sleep?"

"Does she have a crib?"

"Does she have her own crib? Her own room?"

Get through this.

Get through this.

Get through this interrogation.

We are sitting on the mustard-colored couch. It is mostly
dark in the room. The only light is above us, as if we are permanently subject to interrogation beneath it. I want to laugh at how
cliché the questioning sounds.

If I tell her outright that we did not drop our baby, we did not
kick our baby, we never once left our baby unattended, would she
leave us alone? No, she wouldn't. This is her job.

"No," we say in the same tone as we answer her weight at
birth. Seven pounds even. Twenty and a half inches. We did not
drop our baby. We did not shake our baby.

"What about parents? Siblings?"

No, we say, as she fished for more background information.

I suppose I could give her more. For example, she also had a
lot of hair at birth. And her face was the color of eggplant, wrin-
kled and soft from gestating in liquid for nine months, like every
other newborn. And there was a flu epidemic at the hospital. And
it was winter. And I could still feel my toes after the anesthesia
was administered. And I nearly fell asleep from the anti-nausea

medication in the middle of the ten-minute procedure that cut her out of me. None of it relevant. None of it helpful.

"Sometimes it's hard to tell," she continues, "if a baby is shaken. They are crying all the time, at night."

Just ask us. Just fucking ask the question.

"We did not shake our baby," we say to her. I think we are monotone. Maybe we are monotone; maybe we raise our voices in frustration; maybe we stare at her in disbelief. But I think we just understand her need to comply with protocol and want to move on. The social worker continues from shaken baby syndrome to dropped baby syndrome to slapped baby syndrome.

She tells me later that there have been three cases of subdural hematomas on the floor in the past few months. One was a newborn who had accidentally fallen out of his car seat when his uncle was helping his mother to a pediatrician appointment. The baby hadn't been properly latched into the car seat and fell out onto the concrete on his head. My criminal law attorney brain turns on to all the possibilities: Accidental abuse. Unintentional damage. Manslaughter equivalence. Another story I heard, though, was legitimate abuse. A kid had actually been shaken so hard that he would have permanent and severe brain damage with likely disabilities as a result. The alarm again: Intentional harm. Criminal behavior. Reportable.

With the light above us, I remember my days working on capital punishment cases. In my research, I had learned about a nanny who had been sentenced to death for killing the child under her care due to shaken baby syndrome. It had been proved medically that the child died from head and neck injuries consistent with this shaking. A nun was trying to save the inmate's life, claiming it was an accident. Maybe it was. Some experts argue that the medical information proves that it was accidental. Other experts argue that the evidence points to unequivocal guilt due to intent. Twelve jury members or a nine-judge panel with no medical expertise must agree with one or the other. Arbitrary truth finding codified into law.

Several days later, we are required to sign a waiver submitting Abby to full-body radiation, a series of x-rays to determine if there are any broken bones in any part of the body. Standard protocol whenever an infant (or a child of any age) comes into a hospital with an unexplained injury, particularly an unexplained head injury. I had seen enough cases in my short years of practicing criminal law to know that the protocol was necessary.

We sign the paper. We comply.

The Emotional Differential

I learn rather quickly that intraventricular hemorrhages (IVHs) are not uncommon. An "insult" to the body, IVHs are not terribly unexpected in, for example, preemies or even in full-term vaginal deliveries. Medically, an insult is just an event or occurrence that causes damage to a part of the body. Personally, it feels like an abuse of language.

Perhaps the vomiting that preceded the bleed was connected.

Perhaps she has a rare blood disorder, or a clotting disorder. Didn't my mother bruise easily? Did I? Perhaps Abby was exposed to a virus that made her so sick that it burst a blood vessel in her brain when she was crying so relentlessly from the attempted IV placements at the first hospital, or when we walked to the park the other day, or when we went to Target to buy diapers, or when we had that friend come over to meet her, or when everyone passed her around, or when someone forgot to wash his hands before holding her and had a latent cold. Perhaps it was set off when we drove over construction in the road, or when I had difficulty getting the car seat in and out of its latch, or when she was held by someone who was living with someone whose friend's neighbor had hand-foot-and-mouth disease. Maybe I stressed too much during my pregnancy, or I flew too many times, or ate too many pizzas and burgers, or I forgot my prenatal vitamins that one day in my eighth month, or took Tylenol twice to control migraines in my second trimester, or that I was fighting with my husband too much, or that all of the prenatal screening was wrong, or that I had too many ultrasounds, or that I waited too long to have kids, or that the emotional stasis of the world was ready to be ruptured because things were going well with my career.

But Abby is only six weeks old. If she had bled from childbirth, the doctors opine, the bleed would have appeared at birth. Plus, they tell us, since neither forceps nor vacuum suction were used in her delivery, this is most likely not birth trauma. And since I had a full-term delivery with a planned cesarean and plenty of prenatal care, any missed pregnancy complications were highly unlikely.

As the differential list expands, so do my fears, creating an emotional differential—self-diagnosed, self-impacted, and uncontrolled.

And the investigation continues.

Appendicitis

In December 2012, Amir underwent surgery for an emergency appendectomy. What began as a stomachache reminiscent of food poisoning led to fainting on the bathroom floor in the middle of the night. It wasn't until a day later when sharp pain started creeping into his abdomen that we drove to the emergency room.

Amir's parents rushed to the hospital the minute we dropped the word "operation." While he underwent emergency midnight surgery, they sat beside me in the waiting room and paced between chairs.

I couldn't tell them at the time that I just wanted to be by myself in the waiting room. I hugged them with extreme urgency that silently communicated the shared fear that Amir wouldn't be fine. But in truth, I wanted only private contemplation. For the brief and invisible moment while Amir was in surgery, we braided an intangible thread that connected us between waiting room and operating room, between art and science, between creativity and logic, and one that we knew would not be helped with outside noise. Intellectually, I understood their needs. But emotional and intellectual reactions are often poorly matched in medical scenarios.

Amir's appendix was enormous, the largest the surgeon claimed to have ever seen, but he was able to remove it before rupturing. Amir would heal. His parents rejoiced, jumping from their chairs, hugging themselves, hugging me.

Amir was the first person in his immediate family to graduate from college, shortly followed by his sister, who went on to study psychology in graduate school. He grew up in Los Angeles with two hard-working parents embracing the upward climb of the American dream. My mother-in-law worked as a secretary to a rabbi at a Hebrew school; my father-in-law, in insurance. When Amir told his parents he was applying to medical school, they tried to talk him out of it, making sure that he was doing so because he wanted to, not because of what he perceived to be their hopes or some outdated Jewish stereotype. He took out hundreds of thousands of dollars in student loans, moved across the country to New York, and became the doctor he told himself he would become when he was three years old.

That night in the waiting room, though, I watched as his parents put their concerns aside to concentrate on what they believed were mine. It was like watching the machinations of a beloved well-worn watch. I could see each movement, each tick of the clock, each decision made with discernible effort as they generously tried to focus on me. I spent the time in the waiting room convincing them that I knew Amir would be all right. It was probably my job to join them in concern, but I couldn't. Twenty-five years after witnessing the same operation, I still wasn't worried. Neither was Amir.

When we all met Amir in recovery hours later, he was concerned about one thing: measuring his international standing in statistics.

"The surgeon told me it was the longest appendix he'd seen," Amir said, coming out of anesthesia. "There was just a story about one in India, evidently. The longest recorded in the entire country."

"Really?" we said to him.

"*India!*" he repeated, grinning with pride.

We stared at him.

"Was mine bigger?" he asked.

PERHAPS I SHOULD HAVE BEEN more concerned about his appendectomy, though. Surgery, even a basic procedure like this one, always carries with it the risk of infection and death. But it was a surgery that, according to my father, was the "bread and butter" of most general surgical practices, which makes it somewhat less concerning due to its frequent practice. Irrespective of the dangerous realities of surgery, despite basic ones like this, an appendicitis is also one of the most straightforward diagnoses a surgeon can make. What's more, the vestigial appendix is also one of the few unnecessary organs in the body, and when inflamed to the point of removal, there is little debate as to the appropriate action.

Despite the fact that right lower abdominal pain does have a lengthy differential diagnostic list, a good history and physical examination can often pare down that list quickly. It is possible that five minutes following a quick chat with a patient and a short scan, a physician can rule out almost everything on the list and make the diagnosis: appendicitis. The plan? Surgery to remove it. The prognosis? Healing and recovery. Perhaps it was that knowledge that brought us calmness after all.

After Amir's parents left, Amir was already googling "largest appendix removed in India" on his phone. Sure enough, he found it. According to the *Times of India*, it was eighteen centimeters long. He looked over to me, the anesthesia finally wearing off.

"It looks like we tied."

Horses and Zebras

In the late 1940s, physician and professor Dr. Theodore Woodward was teaching a class at the University of Maryland School of Medicine. A former member of the United States Army Medical Corps, Dr. Woodward had spent five years traveling the world for the U.S. Typhus Fever Commission, working in North Africa, New Guinea, Italy, England, France, and the Philippines. He would later become a Nobel Prize nominee for his contribution to eradicating the disease. Following his military discharge, he entered private practice in Baltimore, where he was widely known as one of the founding fathers of the field of infectious disease, a specialty within internal medicine. Despite such a parade of accomplishment, this preeminent scholar, beloved professor, military veteran, and Nobel Prize nominee is perhaps best known for helping to coin one of the most well-known aphorisms in medicine:

When you hear hoof beats, think horses—not zebras.

As the story goes, Dr. Woodward once told one of his classes: "Don't go looking for zebras on Green Street." (Green Street was simply a street near the university.) In other words, don't waste your time looking for something rare, because the probability is that what you are trying to diagnose is not the rare treasure.

This adage stems from the medieval philosophical principle Occam's razor, formulated in the fourteenth century by Franciscan friar William of Ockham, who argued that when deciphering among competing hypotheses, we should select the one that requires the fewest assumptions. While many even more complicated solutions may present themselves or ultimately prove true, in the absence of certainty, the fewer assumptions made, the better. When we apply that same principle to horses and zebras in the medical field, it's remarkable that despite the extraordinary advancements, extended lifespans, artificial limbs, and transplanted organs, we have advanced little conceptually in the better part of a millennium.

While teaching hundreds of future doctors in his long career,

Dr. Woodward knew that most cases would not be solved with a detective's magnifying glass. Instead, they would require the evaluation of all of the data presented followed by analytic reasoning.

When creating a differential, the rule of thumb is not to focus too deeply on trying to find the odd diagnosis. If you see a child with a sore throat, runny nose, cough, green-colored mucus, and red eyes, she probably has a cold. If a patient presents with acute pain on the lower right side of his abdomen with no prior surgeries or any possibility of food poisoning, the diagnosis is likely appendicitis.

A zebra, on the other hand, sounds just like a horse, gallops with hoof beats, and, if your eyesight isn't exactly what it should be, could also appear to be a horse. Zebras are not necessarily known to wander Green Street or any street for that matter, though it is certainly not impossible. It is significant to note that zebras in medicine are not necessarily rare diagnoses; rather, they are *surprising* ones: the diagnoses that may be common, but not to a certain person in a certain season in a certain city with a certain medical history. An eight-year-old girl presenting with lower-right-quadrant pain, for example, is likely suffering from appendicitis, but the zebra could be ectopic pregnancy, a life-threatening pregnancy in which the egg is fertilized in the fallopian tubes—a devastating but not altogether uncommon predicament, only not in an eight-year-old girl. That is both surprising and rare, but possible.

This phrase is so commonly used that physicians and nurses will often speak of the zebras when referring to care as easily as

I would use the word "jurisdiction" in a legal context, or "metaphor" in writing. This idea has become simply part of the language. When doctors create a differential diagnosis, particularly when horses are consistently ruled out, zebras may come into play. Abby's case is no exception.

A rheumatologist, Amir lives his life in this tiny segment of the medical world. His day is filled with the unknown: patients coming in with ailments that likely have no clear answers, with aches, pains, and a long scroll of previously consulted specialists who have been unable to offer an answer, or at least to provide an answer they need. Though many come to him for maintenance of their arthritis, others visit hoping for that last resort, for the answer to the long-standing years of mysterious pain, and there isn't always an answer.

Certain specialties in medicine lend themselves to the unknown. Some internists—specialists in infectious disease, neurology, oncology, and rheumatology, for example—can spend their lives chasing the pearl.

There is an oncological disease called monoclonal gammopathy of undetermined significance (MGUS), in which, broadly speaking, an abnormal protein resides in the blood of the patient. It often presents with no complications or problems, but *can* lead to some types of blood cancers. Though the disease is not cancer, it is a condition that does predispose patients to cancers—and itself connotes a sense of unease and unknowability. The name itself is situated in the abstract—*undetermined significance.* Macmillan Cancer Support, a well-known British charity, even writes about the emotional problems associated with this diagnosis on its Web site: "Although MGUS isn't cancer and most people never develop problems, you may still feel anxious or uncertain at times. These are normal reactions. These feelings usually get easier to cope with over time."

Similarly, the field of neurology covers the broad and developing diagnoses connected with autism. Children on the spectrum often present with features secondary to other neurological diseases, causing neurologists to sometimes question the symptomatological source and diagnosis of autism itself. For example, in past years, the erstwhile diagnosis of pervasive developmental disorder not otherwise specified (PDD-NOS), associated with delays in developmental and social skills, was an uncategorizable diagnosis of a sort of autism disorder that did not fit into any particular end of the spectrum. It was a label to scale certain behaviors difficult to diagnose and categorize. Though the latest *Diagnostic and Statistical Manual of Mental Disorders*, the DSM-5, removed PDD-NOS from its diagnosable disorders in exchange for the umbrella autism spectrum disorder, the over- or under-labeling of unexplained disease and disorders can wreak havoc for those who rely on a name, like the former PDD-NOS, to lend legitimacy to their suffering and treatment.

In the world of obstetrics and gynecology, patients may be forced to confront the dreaded "unexplained infertility" categorization. Medicine simply cannot always provide an answer for what is stopping the egg and sperm from joining as one. A friend experiencing this told me that she was shocked by the name of her diagnosis, or lack thereof. It made her more frustrated that she had nothing to do, nowhere to direct her anger, no actions to carry out apart from the ill-informed advice to "stress less."

And the supremely abstract specialty of rheumatology, which both my sister and husband practice, includes, among other conditions, something called undifferentiated connective tissue disease (UCTD), which is essentially a gray zone of musculoskeletal ailments that do not properly fit into any other clearly definable diagnosis; while they do have some features of clearly definable diagnoses, they lack sufficient clinical features to confirm them. In these fields, physicians are often hunting the obscure, attempting to explain the unexplainable, or finding the occasional zebra.

I spoke with New Jersey rheumatologist Dr. Adrienne Hollander about this phenomenon when she told me about May, a long-term patient of hers in her late fifties, who presented one day in her office with tiny dots on the lower half of her legs, from her knees down to her ankles.

"They looked like pencil-point-sized, black-and-blue dots called petechiae," she told me, clarifying that they were not petechiae—they merely appeared to be so. A constellation of miniature bruises, in essence, was covering the bottom half of her legs. This symptom simply did not fit into her longstanding diagnosis of the autoimmune disease, lupus, for which Dr. Hollander had been treating her for years.

May has suffered from lupus since her early twenties. A potentially life-threatening illness, lupus is a chronic inflammatory disease that occurs when the body's immune system attacks its own tissues and organs. Lupus can attack almost any organ in the body and is a tricky disease because its symptoms often mimic other ailments, making the diagnosis somewhat difficult and the differential rather lengthy.

In May's case, her lupus manifests with chorea, involuntary swooping arm movements that make her seem as though her limbs are swimming through air. Her arms and body sway, and it's as if she is sometimes dancing to music that isn't there. In fact, the term "chorea" comes from the Greek word *choros*, which literally means "dance." May is prone to opening and closing her hands, and has to cross her legs back and forth because she is unable to find a comfortable position. This lupus with chorea has become a debilitating illness that has redefined her life.

There is no cure for lupus, but there are medications that can help regulate its symptoms, and the plan for May worked. For decades, May has been on a cocktail of medications controlling these flares. By the time Dr. Hollander began treating her, she had long since experienced the brutal manifestations of lupus and had resigned herself to a life with the illness. But the dots spread across her legs told an altogether unusual story. They simply didn't fit.

"With lupus, whatever type of inflammation and symptoms patients get in the first five years of the illness will often be the symptoms which remain," Dr. Hollander said. In other words, whatever lupus they start with is the lupus they have over time. It's not like cancer, which spreads, metastasizing in various organs. Any sort of inflammation of blood vessels, which might have explained the petechiae-type bruising, didn't exactly fit with brain inflammation, and because of this unusual presentation, Dr. Hollander couldn't stop thinking about May.

"Her case was rumbling around in my brain," she told me. "Her symptoms weren't presenting as I was used to."

Then, two weeks later, May returned to Dr. Hollander's office, this time with a massive bruise covering her upper inner thigh, from groin to knee. When asked how it happened, May replied, "Nothing happened. It just sort of grew from the last time I saw you."

Dr. Hollander was worried about anemia. A bruise that size could indicate substantial bleeding into her leg, so she ordered additional blood tests and investigated a bit more. Because of her lupus, May was uncomfortable leaving her home. The steroid she had taken for decades to manage her lupus causes her bones to break easily, and so she also has a long history of fractures. She has arthritis and osteoporosis. It's difficult for her to be active, so instead of risking pain and ridicule, she has remained at home with an aide; she rarely goes to the grocery store, instead consuming toast, peanut butter, and pizza as her nutrition. Vegetables rarely cross her lips. These apparently insignificant details become relevant in the search for an answer to this puzzling presentation of symptoms.

While May was in the office, a significant test result returned. May's hemoglobin count was seven, an indication that she was severely anemic. Dr. Hollander sent her to the hospital for a blood transfusion and to see if they could locate the bleeding. She remained there for two days while doctors attempted to solve the mystery. Meanwhile, Dr. Hollander started to recall a chance encounter from years earlier.

"I was called to the hospital on a consult for a separate case and got there a bit early. While I was waiting, a dermatologist was finishing his examination of the same patient." They had both been called in for what looked like petechiae.

"But this isn't petechiae," the dermatologist said to Dr. Hollander. "This is scurvy. I can tell because the dots, the blood vessels, are at the base of hair follicles on the leg."

Dr. Hollander had not heard that before, or since.

What a great pearl, she thought to herself at the time, locking it into her memory, not knowing when or how it would ever be unearthed again. Scurvy, like most antiquated ailments, is a disease of history, a fable of Gilbert and Sullivan, a morality tale for the British Navy of centuries past. Scurvy is one of the oldest diseases known to man, dating back to the Old Testament. In the thirteenth century, the theologian Jacques de Vitry wrote, regarding a sea voyage:

A large number of men in our army were attacked also by a certain pestilence, against which the doctors could not find any remedy in their art. A sudden pain seized the feet and legs; immediately afterwards the gums and teeth were attacked by a sort of gangrene, and the patients could not eat any more. Then the bones of the legs became horribly black, and so, after the greatest patience, a large number of Christians went to rest on the bosom of the Lord.

The disease can be traced from continent to continent throughout history based on an evolution of diet, availability of fruits and vegetables, and understanding of nutrition. Perhaps it is most famous for causing the British Navy of the nineteenth century to rather unfortunately be nicknamed "Limeys," because of the distinct odor of lime emanating on board due to a daily rationing of lime juice to help prevent scurvy. It worked. They were some of the healthiest sailors of the time, helping the British Navy become one of the world's best.

Though biblical in its history and medical significance, it certainly doesn't pop up in the self-defined suburban rheumatology practice of southern New Jersey, where arthritis and osteoporosis are the frequent callers. But after several days, the defining test result came back, and there it was: the answer in all its stripes.

"Her vitamin C levels were basically undetectable," she said to me. "May had *scurvy!*"

The treatment for scurvy is nothing more than high doses of vitamin C and a better diet of fruits and vegetables. It took about a month, but scurvy was soon eliminated from May's body.

Of course, scurvy is not a rheumatologic disease, but it is so rare that it is a perfect representation of the types of abnormal cases that rheumatologists often see. A specialty that is constantly fielding the unknown or extending long differentials, rheumatology sees the basic mechanical problems of arthritis and osteoporosis, but is also the repository for zebras that other fields struggle to diagnose. When rheumatologists hear hoof beats, they think of both horses and zebras.

Amir's years of practice in a world seeking the zebra trained him to accept the unknown. To tell himself to wait for his child's diagnosis and prognosis, if either would even be presented. His patients come in seeking answers, and he must frequently respond, "We may not have one, but we can try to work on eliminating some of what it is not." This doesn't please everyone. It can't. Some patients want a diagnosis, even if it comes with stigma, collateral damage, and a lifetime of medication and maintenance. They hope for the zebras when nothing else remains.

So when Abby is hospitalized, Amir is consciously able to wrap his head around the concept of the NICCU, around the workups from numerous specialists, around the idea that we'll have to wait to find out answers, and then wait some more to find out more answers, and then possibly wait for years to find out the rest. At least on the surface, he is able to accept that we may never have an answer, and is able to retain that sense of reason and levelheadedness that can come across as unemotional and detached at times and empathetic and present at others. The NICCU team is full of practitioners who handle trauma and catastrophic injuries. When they offer head trauma, infection, and bleeding disorders, Amir offers zebras.

Still, despite his background and training, he has no training in pediatrics; he's neither intensivist, neurologist, nor neurosurgeon. He knows this; I know this. It doesn't help the unconscious when, despite being a doctor, you still sit by your daughter's bedside waiting for answers. Waiting to ask questions like any other parent. You know just enough to worry, but not so much that you know how to treat this, how to forecast this, how to diagnose.

When the team comes to Amir, asking for his thoughts on Abby's case, he follows them willingly down any road, contributing zebras and horses specific to his background, and together, they try to eliminate some of what this is not.

Video

When I'm not with Abby in her room, I rewatch the four videos from the previous day on my phone. I cannot help but look to see if something was missed when I showed them to the doctors in haste, or if Amir or I missed something in person that could provide some sort of a clue.

I open one of them. It is 6:47 in the evening on March 12. I film as Amir holds Abby sweetly, every so often speaking to her, calming her with a soft, "Shhhhhh. Are you OK?"

It is probably only an hour or so after I come home from the first ER visit, and that "twitching to keep an eye on" I mentioned earlier to Amir is worsening. Her tiny left hand is almost completely covered with a small circular Band-Aid, hiding the two previous attempts at IV placements. Her right hand, naked without additional dressing for the last time in weeks, is noticeably twitching rhythmically. I direct my hands to hers, grabbing her palm to see if it stops on its own.

Abby stares at me between her calls for help. She is uncharacteristically wearing pink. A pale pink Onesie with a small turquoise bird on her chest, a gift, detracts from her gaze. She does not appear to be in pain when still, at least not great pain. She is not crying consistently, but when she does, her features tie together into a knot of agony.

The video is short, a mere thirty-seven seconds. After a twitch, she cries out in a hoarse voice and then retreats.

"Shhhhhh," Amir says to her.

She is mostly quiet, save for the asynchronous cries that continue to play every few seconds.

"Are you OK?" he says to Abby.

Five simple words usually follow that question, a sentence every parent has uttered to every sobbing child at one point: *Everything's going to be OK.*

Rewatching the video, I try to remember if he said that, if he said anything else after the phone stopped recording.

Philip Roth once wrote that "memories of the past are not memories of facts, but memories of your imaginings of the facts." That I cannot re-create the facts of the past does not change the fact that I still question them. Does Amir calm her as he calms me? Does he look terrified himself? Do I calm him? Will I be the logical attorney directing everyone, or sit passively by, observing detail in full, transcribing all into my memory? Is he going to be playing the role of reassuring, hopeful parent or pragmatic physician?

I want to hear those five simple words, no matter their futility, their fallacy.

Everything's going to be OK.

After pressing play a hundred times on the video, my heart trades places with Abby, and I am wearing the pink cotton Onesie with the turquoise baby bird plastered across my chest, and I am fairly certain that once I stop recording, nothing more is said.

At Least It's Not White

In 2010 I was living in Austin, Texas, where I was a judicial clerk for two years to a judge on the Texas Court of Criminal Appeals. I was writing fiction at night while working as a lawyer during the day. When the clerkship ended, I decided to take a year to focus on my writing full time and complete the novel that had taken over my life for the previous several years. I wanted to feel the psychological free fall of the unknown, the physical fear of having no obvious place to land, so I went skydiving from fourteen thousand feet over the Hill Country of Texas. I had previously gone to graduate school for both creative writing and law, and was governed by my six-figure student loan debt, but never gave myself the chance to focus on my writing, in part because of the loans, in part because of age. This was that chance. The two-year legal clerkship came to a close. I worked on the novel in that time until I moved to Los Angeles in early 2012 and again needed a job. I began working as an associate litigation attorney at a midsize law firm, and when the novel sold to a publisher, I did not quit my day job. I felt committed to the firm for at least another year, so I stayed on until these two parts of my life could no longer coexist. In March 2013, two months before the book was published, I resigned from my legal job to once again embrace the creative life and moonlight as an attorney, instead of the other way around. This time, Amir, my brother, and I drove to Las Vegas to celebrate for the weekend. While there, I dragged Amir and my brother on a roller coaster to celebrate.

The aching thrill of flying through the air, albeit much safer within the confines of an old coaster, was mildly reminiscent of free falling over the wide plains of Texas, and I welcomed it. Amir, on the other hand, wasn't able to. For forty-eight hours following the rickety coaster, he was unable to shake a severe headache. We resumed regular life activities following the celebration, but the severe pain in his head never waned.

"I should probably get a CT scan," Amir told me a day after the ride. "Just to rule out a slow bleed."

He wanted the scan so he'd know if he could take ibuprofen, which he initially refused because anti-inflammatories can exacerbate bleeding. Instead of going straight to a large hospital for more comprehensive care, we opted to skip the long ER lines and just get the scan at the equivalent of a 7-Eleven drive-by local hospital. Only four months earlier, we had spent enough time in a large hospital for his appendectomy. This time, we would go somewhere quickly first, and only continue on to a larger hospital if necessary.

Amir sat for the scan, relaxed but still in excruciating pain. He couldn't move his head without its contents feeling a massive shift inside. I watched from the technician's booth as he captured image after image in the system.

Once complete, Amir asked to see the images while we were awaiting the radiologist's reading. The technician agreed.

Amir stood in shock as he saw a large black splotch on the screen, covering nearly a quarter of his brain.

The technician looked over at us as if we were ghosts. Though each of us was untrained to read the images properly, even the technician must have known that this looked irregular.

"You probably shouldn't be back here," he said to us.

"Just give us a minute," I told him. "We want to see them all."

The images told the story like a 1920s animated flipbook. Flip to the next and the black abnormality grew larger, bleeding outward, it seemed, with each passing image, a wet ink splotch gradually settling into place. Even his skull looked affected, thinner near the edge of the abnormality as though the flick of a finger would erode the remaining bone.

"I'm sorry," the tech said to us. "You really shouldn't be looking at these."

Amir nodded, quickly pulling out his phone to snap a few rudimentary photos of the scans.

We walked back to the examining room in the ER and waited for the attending physician to return with the radiologist's report telling us what this black mass was doing in Amir's brain. It took nearly an hour.

When he finally arrived, the attending couldn't push us out faster. Consult with a neurosurgeon immediately, the discharge papers said. "Neurosurgeon" was spelled wrong.

It was then I learned that white indicated blood on a CT scan. Amir had explained to me that, thank goodness, the mass in his brain was not showing up as white in the image. A bleed that size would have been so catastrophic, it might have killed him. In Amir's CT scan, the repugnant object was black, and although it shouldn't have been there, at least it wasn't white. At least it wasn't blood. At least it wasn't white.

We went home and packed two large bags as quickly and as quietly as possible. We knew it might be some time before we came home. It was the middle of the night, and we didn't call or wake anyone. We sat quietly in the car together and drove to the larger hospital.

We spent the remainder of the night in a single hospital bed, being awakened by nurses every thirty minutes to ensure that Amir was still alive, that his pain was manageable, and that he was going to be able to go to his MRI at eight a.m. the following morning. We cuddled together that night, his comforting six-foot-three frame curling my five feet and barely one inch, just as we had done four months earlier while recuperating from his appendectomy in what might as well have been the same hospital bed.

Hours before sliding into an MRI scanner to learn if he may

need brain surgery, if he might have cancer, if he might lose his personality, mobility, intelligence, or life, he was still playing the role of comforting spouse and objective physician, as if his embrace would shroud us both in certainty. He needed that. He needed to focus on his training in order to get through the night. But I did not. Just as a person grows older and realizes that her parents aren't perfect, so, too, did I realize that my reliance on medicine had been naïve, innocent. It wasn't a pure erosion of its dependability, but rather that for the first time, I was staring at something potentially catastrophic without having a clear plan in place. This wouldn't necessarily be as easily cut out as tonsils or tumors on less vital organs, and carried with it much greater questions of a future, and even larger questions of a past. We rested in bed together, my fingers touching his appendectomy scars, still barely healed. We held each other and spoke about our joys and sadness, our work, our frustrations and triumphs, our longing to start a family, until morning came and the room was once again filled with family, doctors, and nurses. Though I still believed that appendectomies were nothing to worry about, I was sure that I had failed him in my spousal concern some sixteen weeks earlier. His persistent pain was excruciating, far worse than the appendicitis. He was wheeled out for a quick MRI— without need for anesthesia or intubation—and back in a short hour later, when the neurosurgeon arrived with a prognosis and diagnosis in hand.

"It's just an arachnoid brain cyst," he said with little interest.

He was generous in his time and patient in his explanations.

We quickly learned that arachnoid brain cysts are not uncommon and often have no side effects or effect on longevity or general health. In fact, most people who have them don't even know they have them because people don't typically have brain scans without cause. Instead, they live full and normal lives without any disruption by these unruly cysts. Those whose brain cysts are problematic show signs of seizures and neurological concerns from an early age. Amir fit into neither category.

"The roller coaster probably just knocked a little cerebrospinal fluid out of it," the neurosurgeon said. "The pain will subside, but you should take it easy for at least another week."

While the cyst was benign and congenital (he'd likely had it since birth), we simply never knew about it. The doctor advised that it was best not to do anything about it, as it wouldn't hinder his life. There wasn't a required follow-up scan, not even a follow-up appointment. Just a prescription of time off from work to allow the fluid to reabsorb into the brain and then get back to his life as if this didn't happen. As if you didn't know you have a brain cyst. As if more knowledge is certainly better than none.

Until March 12, I was sure that Amir wished he never knew about the cyst. But after that day, it became one of the few facts that brought us calmness and insight. We had no idea at the time that every neurologist and neurosurgeon we would visit would scoff at the simplicity and benignity of an arachnoid brain cyst just under a year later while examining the MRI images of Abby's brain.

"Could this be genetic?" we both ask, during the duplicitous medical histories taken daily at Children's Hospital. "Her father has an arachnoid brain cyst."

"No," they each reply independent of one another, as if an arachnoid brain cyst is just a stuffy nose. "Those are pretty common. This is something entirely different."

Degrees

Following Abby's first MRI in the NICCU, Neurology comes to us to review the results, telling us that the story is more complicated. The neurologist can see that there is blood in the brain tissue, not just within the ventricles. It's barely there, but barely is still something. She tells us that the bleed probably started in the tissue and then bled into the ventricles because they are empty spaces for the blood to collect.

And thankfully so, she says with a glimmer of hope. In an infant brain, the ventricles are much larger and can hold more fluid, so the outcome is better. It is preferable to have a place for the blood to flow. A positive and a negative. A fear and a loss. An elevation of diagnosis, with a respite of age.

This sliver of a bleed, the barely-there dripping of blood into the brain tissue, though, elevates the injury to a fourth-degree bleed, the one that carries with it unregulated statistics. And so on we go, still trying to understand why this happened, this injury that carries with it another new slice of language: *periventricular*. *Peri*, just to the side of, the ventricles, and still we don't know why.

The Tell-Tale Heart

When I was in the sixth grade and living in New Orleans, my school had an annual overnight trip to a campsite for middle-schoolers. Along with our Mardi Gras float, the outing was the highlight of the school year. Our parents would willingly sign our permission slips and pack sleeping bags for a hundred-person sleepover that was well known to conclude with a late-night screening of the 1961 film adaptation of *The Pit and the Pendulum*. Adolescent lore claimed that the film would instill terror in all who watched it, and I was fairly certain that I was going to skip out on the film lest I spend the next three months of my life in fear. My mother advised me that I could stay home if I wanted, but after great deliberation I made the decision. I wasn't going to miss this, the main event of the sixth grade.

So I went on the overnight field trip and watched *The Pit and the Pendulum*, in part through my fingers and in part looking over my shoulder when I turned around to face the trees. In my memory, it was midnight and the black sky was dominant. I realize now that it couldn't possibly have been so late. The parameters of this overnight field trip may have mythologized over time, but specific moments from that evening flicker around my subconscious whenever I am afraid. Whenever I feel like I'm staring into an unknown or waiting for the pendulum to swing back and forth to where I want it to be, I see it. Trees, endless trees standing proudly above a darkened sky on one side, and on the other, a Technicolor frame of a man who had been buried alive behind a wall, his ridiculous skeletal prop frozen in asphyxia. Had I watched the film today, I would probably have laughed.

At ten or eleven, though, I wasn't ready to embrace this form of entertainment. I didn't see the artistry in creating anxiety for the viewer at such a young age, and I suspect that this type of field trip today might have little impact on the audience members. Nevertheless, it was my first introduction to Edgar Allen Poe, and it was far from a welcome one.

The first time I read a short story by Poe was a few years later, in high school English class. "The Tell-Tale Heart." I didn't realize at the time how much I would grow to love dark psychological tales such as these, worlds in which our human psyche is far more horrifying and poisonous than a slash of gore. The most perilous safe room, after all, is our own minds. It is there where guilt, which may have manifested from nothing, or perhaps even something real, expands. Worlds created by Poe, by Shakespeare, by Mary Shelley allow us to slit open the skin of our souls and expose our greatest fears.

After the outdoor screening of *The Pit and the Pendulum*, I was afraid of Edgar Allen Poe, but not of blood. I had recently seen a live operation. I had held an electric knife in my hands without realizing what it was when it was turned on. I had grabbed a scalpel from my father's hands when he was helping my mother with an ingrown toenail and saw my fingers grow thick with color. I was far more afraid of what the blood represented than of its visibility, the surgical cutting of flesh. After all, blood is the proverbial symbol of something more severe, something larger than just redness. The true horror, Poe explores, is in the *partial* knowledge, and it is this that can lead to possible guilt and ultimately madness.

Anyone who has ever been sick or related to someone sick has felt this form of guilt at one point or another. The questioning, the partial knowledge causing you to think that you may be at fault, or the nagging suspicion that someone may think you are at fault. When your responsibility is to keep your child safe and you fail, there is nowhere else to turn but your own psyche, screaming at you—a self-imposed punishment far worse than any other kind.

In "The Tell-Tale Heart," Poe explores the psychology of a man descending into madness over killing an innocent man. Though based in actual guilt, his subconscious guilt overtakes him, transforms him, turning him mad. "My head ache[s]," Poe writes in his narrator's voice. "And I fanc[y] a ringing in my ears . . . It continued and became more distinct . . . until, at length, I found that the noise was not within my ears." By the time the narrator in the story is nearly free from liability, it is clear he is nowhere near cleansed of his guilt. His cadence changes swiftly; he speaks fast. He fills the space with words, pressured and airy. He raves; he swears, exhibiting the tell-tale signs of guilt.

If we think we've done something wrong, even if it is untrue, even if it is irrational or beholden to forces outside our control, our neuroses tell this story in our physicality. And doesn't that then become our story, or at least a part of it? We are our own guilt. We become our own guilt, regardless of merit or logic. It is this quality that makes us human. It is a defining absentia in sociopaths. Given that fact, we should be grateful for our guilt, even if it is at times unreasonable. We should nourish it, tend to it, try to understand it, because it is that little fact-checking safeguard keeping us from making bad decisions, separating us from sociopaths, reminding us that we are human. It is our beating tell-tale heart.

Nobody knows this sentiment more than a parent whose child is sick.

"Forensics"

Somewhere near the third full day in the NICCU, a young doctor named John wanders into our room. He can't be older than twenty-nine, thirty maybe, wearing jeans and a white coat, as if he is trying to be the cool doctor, the friendly doctor, the one we are supposed to confide in. John is a nice enough guy. He introduces himself by his first name, as if that is supposed to ingratiate himself to us, and then tells us he's from CARES.

"CARES?" we ask, exhausted by this next round of questioning. "What field is that?"

"It's a group that focuses on the patient," he says.

He is smiling, gesturing with his hands like a friend.

"Yes, but what specialty?" we ask.

"We're part of forensics."

"But what *specialty*?" we insist.

He doesn't reply. The stock answers have been provided.

"What subspecialty? What kind of doctor are you working with? Pediatrics? Surgery? Neonatology? ID? What?"

He still says nothing.

"You're a resident on rotation to find out if we hurt our baby, aren't you?" we both say to him.

He tries to respond, awkwardly agreeing. A few seconds pass. Neither one of us speaks, but nobody looks away.

"I have to ask these questions," he says eventually.

Amir and I don't need to review it again.

"Let's just get it over with," we say.

He goes through the rote questionnaire.

Had you x, had you y, did you z at any point in time?

No, no, no, no, and no.

I later learn from the hospital's Web site that "the CARES Team is the only child abuse team in Southern California, and perhaps the nation, with board-certification in both child abuse and in developmental-behavioral pediatrics (as well as in general pediatrics), providing a critical additional focus, and enabling a more comprehensive assessment in all child abuse cases."

I stopped taking all medications, save my daily thyroid pill and prenatals. My skin broke out terribly, but I refused to take any topicals or medications because I was pregnant. I didn't drink alcohol or caffeine. I didn't eat soft cheeses or deli meats or sushi or sunny-side-up eggs or meat that wasn't fully cooked. I even stopped running when I felt cramping. I did travel extensively but canceled trips toward the end of my pregnancy when I started feeling Braxton-Hicks contractions.

I don't say any of this, of course. The specifics never come up. He doesn't ask.

Questions fly by us, old and new. By the time he visits us, the story has been retold in so many ways that it feels cold, stale, inhuman. Were we unknowingly tweaking the important facts for each doctor, lending our own filter of significance to them? That's the problem with medical histories. Patients are notoriously bad historians. Even the ones who practice medicine and tell stories for a living. Eyewitnesses to our own lives, even we fail. Facts are forgotten, left out, misinterpreted, unknown to be significant.

"I hear you may have been sick, too?" he says, looking directly at me. "How are you feeling?"

Nobody has asked about me or Amir once, and I haven't volunteered any information. This isn't about me. Nothing right now is about me. Even if I have felt a little queasy over the previous few days, it is easily explained. I'm six weeks postpartum. The day I visited my OB for my first postpartum visit, Abby fell ill.

But John's eyes survey my face, inspecting it, as if I'm leaving something out of the story, a story I had told a million times in two days, a story I know as well as—

"How long have you had that cold sore?" he asks.

I think about it. "It just started a day ago," I say. We've been in the hospital for over a day now, too. "I hadn't been feeling great for a few days, but nothing so bad."

"Uh-huh," he says, writing down something in the notes.

He isn't talking about Abby being dropped anymore.

"You're good historians," he tells us, after completing the questionnaire and all three of our medical histories.

Amir puts his arm around me and I put mine around him, but the blame is quickly shifting from us to me.

Somewhere in my memory's attic, I remember that cold sores can spread. They are part of the herpes simplex virus. They can spread to the eyes, causing blindness. They can spread to the brain, causing inflammation. My head aches and a ringing in my ears haunts my consciousness with such noise that I can't think. The beating heart inside my chest becoming louder, louder, louder.

Then, the resident asks a few more questions and states a few more medical facts, none of which I remember. All I can remember is feeling my body fold into itself, origami-like. A contortionist without joints.

I suspect my voice is pressured, my countenance panicked. Had I been arrested on the spot or interrogated by any social worker or John the forensics guy, my temperament at the moment would surely have been used against me. In the hospital, though, there are no floorboards under which to hide. No way to dismember my fears.

I leave the room and run to the elevators until I make it to the ground floor wanting to leave, but unable. I haven't called a single friend yet. I haven't even spoken on the phone with my sister or brother. I spoke with my parents briefly, but even their voices couldn't comfort me. I don't want to tell them about this possibility.

"There's a chance that it could be connected," I hear echoing from the CARES doctor, from Infectious Disease, from Neonatology, from Pediatrics, and from Amir over the course of the next week.

It's possible this is HSV. She'll need a spinal tap for the test, but we'll start her on antivirals until the results come back just to be proactive. Just to make sure we're covering all the bases.

And that's when I remember it. I had heard "HSV" called out in the emergency room several days earlier. I heard "encephalitis" listed in that short differential in the emergency room by a physician who took a three-second look at me, knowing, *It's you; it's you. It's all your fault.*

Out, Damned Spot!

The days waiting for the HSV test results to return transmit slowly. I find myself unable to sleep at night. I lie behind the curtain in Abby's room, keeping my distance. I pump breast milk at two in the morning, at six in the morning, hoping to be awake for her seven a.m. visit from the neurosurgeon, after which I will continue pumping breast milk. That, I can give her, regardless of what else I have shared. I wander the hallways, sometimes speaking with night nurses, sometimes with other parents. But because she needs additional testing in the form of a spinal tap, Abby is intubated and ventilated for additional days beyond the MRI, with a machine breathing for her, keeping her alive. I love and hate medicine in this moment. It is at once natural—the breath inhaling and exhaling in rhythmic time—and unnatural. A requisite element of life brought upon by mechanics and technology.

Meanwhile, the spot on my lip grows larger in my mind, beating like a heart, spilling like fresh blood, my literary metaphors mixing, keeping me awake. I become Lady Macbeth overnight. Unable to sleep, I walk the grounds of the hospital as she walks the grounds of her castle in a daze, repeatedly trying to wash the blood from her hands, silently crying, "Out, damned spot! Out, I say." Every time I pass an antibacterial box, I squeeze two or three drops and rub them in until the skin on my hands splits. Dryness, peeling, the revelation of my own blood peeking out from the broken skin, the dried-up lifelines in my palms. *Out, damned spot.*

I walk to the bathroom, and every nurse who passes me sees it. I am sure of this. I sit in the family room where every parent who waits here, hoping for a miracle for his or her child, looks at me, no doubt thinking it is me, blaming me, because I did this. I did this to my own child. I kissed my own child and caused her brain to inflame.

Out, damned spot. Out, I say! Off my face, off my lips. I want to kiss Amir. I want to kiss Abby. I can kiss neither.

"At least if it turns out positive," Amir says, "they'll give her antivirals and she'll get better. We'll have an answer."

As he views his wife's mounting madness, Macbeth asks the doctor to "Cure her of that!" Cure his wife of the madness, the guilt, the sleepwalking, the incessant hand washing, the need to wipe clean her hands from the spots of red blood she sees upon them.

> Canst thou not minister to a mind diseased,
>
> Pluck from the memory a rooted sorrow
>
> Raze out the written troubles of the brain.
>
> And with some sweet oblivious antidote
>
> cleanse the stuffed bosom of that perilous stuff
>
> which weighs upon the heart?

Is my "mind diseased"? Am I turning mad? Does Amir see it? Does everyone on the floor see it, too? The doctor in *Macbeth* suggests that "the patient must minister to himself." And yet, the doctor in my head, the doctor in my bed, replies, *You didn't do anything wrong. Even if you did this, you did nothing wrong.* How could he and I both be right? If I was guilty of hurting her, even if unintentional, it does not absolve me from the guilt. Perhaps blame, but not guilt. It's a personally abusive form of Schrödinger's Cat.[1] The

---

1. Schrödinger's Cat is a thought experiment formulated by Nobel Prize–winning Austrian physicist Erwin Schrödinger, which broadly states that the act of observing something

minute we open the box, the minute the test results come back, the answer will be revealed. I can't have done this and not done this at the same time. I can't be guilty and innocent together.

I can only wash my hands, cleanse my face, and walk the halls searching for a breast pump to express milk for Abby for when she might come off the respirator. Because she might come off it. She would come off it. She has to. I clean my hands and delicately observe Abby from a distance. Rinse. Repeat. Pump. Rinse. Repeat. Pump. Just pump. Pump milk. Pump ounces of bottles until my breasts bleed dry.

Get Out!

Amir is being questioned privately by a third social worker when it happens.

I am in the family room speaking with two other parents while I wait for them to finish. Periodically, I look at my phone, waiting for a text from Amir to let me know when he's done. There is no text and enough time passes alone in the family

changes it. To demonstrate this theory, Schrödinger placed a cat in a box with a hammer, a small amount of radioactive material that had only a fifty percent chance of decaying, poison, and a counter. The setup: If the counter detected the decaying of the radioactive material, it would emit radiation, causing the hammer to smash the poison, killing the cat. And quite simply, if the counter did not detect the radiation, it would not smash it, keeping the cat alive. The outcome: If an observer opened the box to view the experiment in process, it would be impossible to predict the cat's natural outcome. As a result, the conclusion is that until the box is opened, the cat exists in a state of being both alive and dead.

room with no more Malaysian airplane news, so I walk back through the unit to our room. The questioning with Amir cannot have taken that long.

But when I walk into the room, Amir is sitting in the darkness alone. At first, I don't realize what is in his hands. I only see the empty incubator pulled away from the wall. The wires are still attached to Abby's chest and fingers and toes, only now she is in Amir's hands for the first time since walking into the emergency room nearly a week earlier.

She is quietly sleeping in his arms. Two months later, she weighs the same as she did at birth.

I gasp.

"You're *holding* her?"

It's hard to say the word "holding," as if it is a word I can no longer pronounce properly.

He doesn't reply. His eyes are closed and nothing anyone could say would open his arms to release her to me.

"How long?" I ask. "Why didn't you call me?"

He looks up as if awakening to his life.

"I just needed a moment."

HOURS LATER, when I am holding Abby in my arms trying to reestablish a proper latch for nursing, Amir tells me how his third interrogation ended. In the middle of the questions, though, Abby's primary neonatologist returned to the room and unhooked a few wires, allowing her to be lifted out of the incubator. It was time.

"I couldn't talk anymore," he says. When the umpteenth social worker danced around the question of her injury, he lost his normal monotone and composure. He had to stop it. He knew that they'd be writing something cruel and judgmental in their reports if he lost his temper during their interview, but it was enough. Three feet away, Abby's doctors were picking her up. She was doing well enough now that she could be held.

By the time the medical questions shifted into legal ones, Amir finally asked, "Is this to ask if I dropped my child? Because the previous social worker has already gone over that, as did your forensics expert. I think you know how clear it is that I have not. We're done now. I'm going to hold my child. Please leave."

"Just a few more—"

"Get out!" he shouted.

And she complied.

Five minutes later, I walked in.

Part of me is jealous that he got to hold Abby first. I carried her for nine months. I went with her to the first ER. I allowed rashes to sprout all over my skin instead of taking medications while pregnant. I refused cheese and caffeine and alcohol and adrenaline. I was cut open with a scalpel to have four foreign hands pull her from my warm womb. I produce the milk. I nourish her. I should hold her first.

But we are still waiting for the test results, and so it's right that he gets to hold her before me. He can kiss her, after all. I cannot. Even if all of this was unintentional, at least it wasn't his fault.

THE *OXFORD ENGLISH DICTIONARY* defines guilt as "a failure of duty, delinquency"; or an "offence, crime, sin." It is the "responsibility for an action or event; the 'fault' *of.*" Its many other definitions also include "sin" and "crime" and "liability," but not once does the *OED* include the word *blame* in its extensive etymology, which is instead defined as "the action of censuring; *expression* of disapprobation; *imputation* of demerit on account of a fault or blemish; *reproof; censure*; reprehension. A charge, an accusation. Culpability; fault. Responsibility for anything wrong, culpability."

Blame is the act of imparting culpability. Anyone who is blameworthy will not necessarily experience guilt. The inverse isn't always true. Those septic with blame often fail to realize it, an altogether distinct problem. Still, though blame and guilt are cut from the same cloth of wrongdoing, they do not lay claim to each other. Blame is expressly pointing the finger; it is the action; it is charging someone with liability, telling her that she is culpable, that he may be guilty. Guilt, meanwhile, is an internal wrestling with your demons as you ask yourself, *Did you fail to do something right? Did you fail to protect yourself? Did you fail to protect your child?*

While waiting for results, there is nothing to do but think about this. Find that finger and point it somewhere. The inward arrow is directed toward the self. The outward inevitably comes later.

. . .

ACCORDING TO THE JOHNS HOPKINS Health Library, cold sores infect upwards of 50 to 80 percent of the population. The National Institutes of Health (NIH) estimates that 90 percent of adults will be exposed to the virus by the age of fifty. The uncommon fact: cold sores can, albeit infrequently, cause brain inflammation.

This isn't an unfounded fear, but rather a leading contender on every doctor's differential diagnosis. Part of me wants it to be true so that Abby will have an answer and treatment—a known drug with a known result, which will lead to a known resolution, so we can go home and focus on healing and rehabilitation. But the other part of me actually hopes for a negative result, for the continuation of our uncertainty, so I will be absolved from actual blameworthiness. But I can't have both. I know that. Schröding-er's Cat is merely a thought experiment, a paradox in full.

The comprehensive scans reveal that Abby has no broken bones, no signs of trauma, no trauma of any form. The bleed, we know from the images, also started on the inside of the brain, not near the skull, so it wasn't even the type of injury that could result from being hit or dropped or shaken. She doesn't have a scrape, cut, or bruise on any part of her body, apart from the yellowing marks where blood draws had been attempted the previous day.

The social worker never apologizes. I can't blame her. It's her job. The last time we see her, she gives us free parking permits for one week.

After forty-eight hours, the test results come back negative. What's more, the neurosurgeon says the bleed cannot possibly be due to HSV because the blood pattern is not consistent with that diagnosis.

For two very conclusive reasons, I am in the clear.

Abby still isn't.

The Intangibles

A dear friend of mine, Kendall, has a gorgeous daughter named Emery, just over a year older than Abby. Emery was diagnosed in the second month of her life with a very rare tumor called a melanotic neuroectodermal tumor of infancy (MNTI). It's a "shit happens" sort of diagnosis, Kendall has often told me. Why people get cancer, why babies get sick, we don't often know. But as parents, of course, we blame ourselves despite our intellect and common sense refuting it. And when something inexplicable happens to our children, guilt and blame become muddled.

Kendall and I share every fear and every consequence over the course of both of our children's hospitalizations, and I was well aware that many people she was close to made her feel even more guilty for things beyond her control, merely because she was the parent. It was not explicit finger pointing. There were no proverbial villagers coming to the castle to intentionally blame her for what was happening. Rather, it was little sediments of external concern, unhinged commentary, unfiltered words from friends and family trying to figure out what went wrong, as if they could do it with their limited knowledge.

When she heard, "We're praying for Emery because we know you don't pray, and so we'll pray for you," she heard, *It's because you don't pray that this happened.*

When someone asked, "Do we know what caused it?" She questioned every single aspect of her life, as if there was some unknown activity she did that led to this moment. Of course, there was no unknown activity that led to this.

When someone else asked innocently if it was something that happened during pregnancy, she couldn't help but blame herself, question every action, every detail of her pregnant life, starting to wonder, too.

Over the phone (as we live in different cities), though, I would picture a group of hopeful parents and grandparents, friends and colleagues, all offering their truths to her, each one of them unknowingly carving a hollow cleft of pain into her back. To think that people close to her were making such painful and yet seemingly altruistic allegations at a time she needed them most was a crueler punishment.

The unknowable reality for all is often too unbearable, so it transforms into a greater self-imposed punishment of abstractia, the place where you pin the illness on yourself. A place that is unprovable, unknown, but still resides in your subconscious like a fly caught between two windowpanes.

The problem is expounded by the fact that many of these

comments come from people who care. They are phrases with the best of intentions that through the machinations of human emotions are twisted and turned like language out of a lawyer's mouth, and placed in the heart of the patient (or parent) with pure cognitive dissonance. You don't want to be angry with someone for caring enough to ask questions, but their comments may be so insensitive that they do nothing but add stress to an already stressful time. I am certain that I was guilty of this, too, no matter how much I wanted to help.

Shortly after her diagnosis, Emery underwent an experimental maxillofacial surgery. Part of her gum was removed where teeth would eventually need to grow. The surgeons were able to extract all precancerous tissue with an excellent prognosis.

Over a year later, I ask Kendall if she still feels guilty now that Emery is doing so well.

"We have a gift in that we know what Emery had," she says to me, "but the guilt has never gone away, because we don't know *why* she got sick."

I didn't realize she'd been torturing herself because of an unknown source, an impossible fact to learn. I know that nothing I say will take that away from her.

"I'm much more accepting of it now and if there was something I did to contribute to it, I didn't knowingly do it, and so I've been able to forgive myself to an extent. But I don't think I'll ever fully forgive myself. It's always in the back of my mind and it randomly pops up."

"When does it pop up?" I ask her.

"Whenever I'm around her," she says to me. My heart begins to crack.

"Because there is a visible reminder that is becoming more and more prominent as she gets older," she says about the part of Emery's gums that was removed, "I feel the guilt every day. The more prominent it is, the more guilty I feel. And nothing will take it away unless I know what caused it."

Emery is now cancer free but faces an uphill battle with reconstructive dental surgeries, including procedures that have never been performed in the United States. And so now they wait, wondering how it will materialize, and where to go. And while they wait, Kendall guilts herself into blame where none exists. It doesn't seem right, but it's like trying to catch a sound wave with a butterfly net. It is far more difficult to forgive yourself when the blame is intangible.

The Rabbi

When she can't send flowers to Abby's room due to NICCU policy, my sister-in-law, Yael, sends her rabbi instead. Her Chassidic, Orthodox rabbi, whom I had met only once before, is our first visitor. This man, with whom we had very little connection—spiritual, personal, or otherwise—leaves his family and comes to the hospital to . . . well, for what we aren't quite sure. Comfort is an option, though it is difficult for me to feel comforted by someone I don't know. Create a space for us to process recent events by waxing philosophical about the precariousness of life? Serve as someone to confide in as if we are hiding something and need to confess before it's too late? Platitudes are far from our needs.

Before visiting hours end, though, the rabbi hands us gifts and prayer books and a small laminated prayer for the sick, asking us to place it in Abby's crib. On one side is a photograph of an aging rabbi, traditional in his observant garb. We are not Orthodox Jews. We are cultural Jews. We keep a kosher home but eat what we like on the outside. We go to synagogue occasionally, but still want to send Abby to Jewish preschool. Heritage is important, cultural affiliation vital, as it represents a connection to our past. Jewish community and tradition defines so much of my identity, but a precise focus on God is far less present. I don't think about religion while at the hospital. I don't make deals with God in exchange for her full recovery. I never make deals with God.

Amir and I look at the baseball card nervously.

"What do we do with this?" Amir asks me once he leaves.

I shrug. "I don't know."

I'm not comfortable assigning one individual so much power.

He shrugs, too.

"I don't know, either."

We walk back to Abby's room with the prayer book and the card dangling from my fingers off a metal chain. Neither of us wants to display it. It doesn't represent our ideals, particularly if praying in this precise way is supposed to bring forth some sort of a miracle.

The word "miracle" disarms me. It assumes that actions taken by human beings are moot, that extraordinary things can't happen from the hand of a friend, a sibling, a parent, a teacher, a doctor, a nurse. Though it is hard to fully deflect the unknowable power of miracles, and even I sometimes refer to them haphazardly in my everyday speech, I still prefer to believe that if my outcome is good or bad, it is so because of an aggregation of life. Selecting miraculous hope for this one individual would make it true for everyone else on the ward, and I know that this can't be true. We aren't making deals with God. We don't blame God or ask God to heal our child, but at the same time, we cannot dispose of the card. There is Hebrew writing on it. A rabbi gave it to us. The karmic inference would be less than ideal. The tiny percentage that I'd be flicking away a speck of goodwill would be the particle of doubt I would hold on to if something went wrong.

We both agree to place it in her crib, along with the stuffed animal and Get Well Soon card from my nieces and my sister, Arielle.

"Far be it from me to stomp on good wishes," I say.

"It's a good faith gesture that she'll heal," Amir says.

Right, we both think.

We sit beside the crib looking in, trying not to laugh at ourselves. Trying not to laugh in disbelief. Trying not to lose faith in the doctors, in the system, in Abby's health, in our health, in ourselves. The term "good faith" has as little to do with religion as it does to negotiations, business contracts. I used to use it frequently in the practice of law to convince people to be persuaded to my side.

I suppose it would be far worse to push away prayers just because they were not requested.

Mashed

The bleed is finally stabilized after over a week in the hospital. For that week, our residence has been the yellow couch beside her bed. But with progress and an answer or two, we finally allow a few visitors. Amir's parents, his sister, my brother, my aunt. I know the geography of the hospital, the location of all the extra breast pumps, the menu in the cafeteria. Amir even returns to work. I tell him in no uncertain terms that he is unemotional, that he is wrong to return to work when our daughter is still in the intensive care unit healing from an injury that could leave her and our futures unclear.

He interprets all of this as me telling him he is a bad father. He has just opened up his own solo medical practice. He has no time off, nobody to cover for him, and if he takes another week off, he will likely lose his business. So reluctantly, he returns to work. He is driving an additional two hours back to the hospital every evening following a day of seeing his own patients. Intellectually I understand his departure, but it doesn't make it easier on me, on our need to remain unified during this acute crisis.

Amir had dreamed of fatherhood since childhood. He longed to be a young father, running around town with a baby or two strapped to his chest. When extra time was available to us, we used to bicker about the superficial ways to pass it: whether we should spend time going for a run or a hike together, exploring the unknown neighborhoods of our city, to read, go to the theater, movies, learn how to cook, spend time with friends and family. When I teased him about lacking hobbies to round out his interests, his response was always the same: "I think it's going to be our kids' hobbie. Plus, I'm excited about doing all those boring weekend chores with them and taking them to parties."

But when he fails to publicly display his emotions by Abby's bedside, his response is logical, precise.

"They know I'm a doctor," he says to me. "And they're talking to me privately, telling me their theories, and actively engaging me in Abby's case like a member of the team. If they see me break down, they may not do that, and I need them to do that. We need them to keep telling us what's going on because maybe we can offer them something to help. If they see me crying by her bed, they may think I've lost objectivity."

"Which you have," I remind him. "You *are* her father. You *are* emotionally subjective about her case."

"This is medicine," he says. "I need to appear objective. I want to keep getting all the extra information, which I can then relate to you. At the hospital, I need to be strong. You can break down by her bedside. I can't."

"I hate that," I say with fury.

"What?"

"The stereotype. It looks like I'm the histrionic mother when

I'm actually handling things quite rationally. You're emotional, too. You just aren't showing it."

"Of course I'm not!" he says. "That's what I can do. You're telling everyone you're a lawyer. You're not introducing yourself as a writer. You're introducing yourself as an attorney. And you sleep in your law school sweatshirts for Christ's sake!"

"I don't even know why I'm doing that," I say.

Begrudgingly, I take his outstretched hand.

I know exactly why I am doing that.

"Look, this is all I can do. I have to," he says to me, his eyes spilling open.

We both want as much attention on her case as possible.

"If she was in jail," Amir says, "I'd be breaking down and you'd be taking over, refusing to show too much emotion, speaking to the police and judges and attorneys."

I'd like to think he's right.

Once home, though, the rigid scaffolding holding Amir's bones together unhinges. He is away from the scouring eye of the nurses and doctors, administration and fellow parents. And he is away from me when it happens.

He is home, reheating some old potatoes—something mashed and stocked in the fridge—and he loses all concept of time. While waiting the forty-five seconds to have warm potatoes from the microwave, he thinks about the fact that Abby is so sick, she might die. She might have developmental problems. She might have more seizures. And like all parents, he simply wants to know why and how. How did he fail her? How did he allow this to happen? Hadn't he been overcautious? Hadn't he requested every family member who visited to get inoculated with both the flu and TDAP vaccines? Hadn't he carefully transferred her body to each friend who wanted to hold her?

By the time he finishes the first rush of questions, the forty-five seconds pass on the microwave, but he is unaware. He pushes the buttons another time. Forty-five more seconds.

How did he fail her? He needs to know. His only job is to keep her safe, keep her healthy, and he couldn't even do that—as a doctor, no less.

And there it is, again: the passing of forty-five seconds on the microwave. A blaring *beep-beep-beep* reminding him of an ambulance siren, of a crisis, the completion of a task.

And again, forty-five more seconds turn the Tupperware around in circles, melting the potatoes until they are solids no more.

Beep-beep-beep.

Opening the microwave to a milky sea of starch, he grabs the Tupperware, and scorching hot in his hands, it drops to the floor, splattering on the tiles in white foamy waves.

An Abbreviated History of Fever

Overnight, Abby develops a fever of 105. Her eyes sink. Her skin is so flush that it actually looks like flames are waving at us beneath the surface in cruel and unusual formations. When I touch her, my fingertips burn. Her body cries out with fire. She drops ounces, weighing less than she did at birth seven weeks earlier. Her body is hollow in my arms and heavy with untold narrative. I feel the temperature in her body rise. She is living in heat. Her torso sweltering, but curiously, her hands and feet freezing, like two bodies sewn together, not meant to be one.

IN THE FIFTH CENTURY BC, the Greek philosopher and physician Hippocrates concluded that disease was generally seen as some sort of imbalance in or disturbance of the natural state of the body. In his treatise *Tradition in Medicine*, which has become one of the foundational texts for modern medicine, Hippocrates contends that the doctor's role is to combat disease by evening out that imbalance until all parts of the body are properly aligned.

Hippocrates describes the body as a composition of four types of humors, within which that balance of health and purity rests: blood, phlegm, black bile, and yellow bile, each corresponding with a primary organ and representing not only physical properties but also emotional disposition.

For example, blood covers the sanguine humor, which is produced by the liver. Its mystical element is air, its qualities are hot and moist, and it produces a red-cheeked individual who is generally happy, generous, optimistic, amorous, and irresponsible. This archetype is one we all know well. Phlegm is the phlegmatic humor, produced by the lungs. Its mystical element is water, and its qualities are cold and moist. A corpulent, sluggish, pallid, and cowardly archetype, the phlegmatic is a less idealistic character archetype, to say the least. Yellow bile represents the choler, largely produced by the spleen. With a mystical element of fire, choleric folks are hot and dry, red-headed and thin, and can be violent, vengeful, short-tempered, and ambitious. And finally, we have the melancholics, derived from the body's black bile, the gall bladder. Their element is the earth; they are cold and dry, and sallow, introspective, sentimental, and thin.

These four humors read like tarot cards, a presumptive collection of old stereotypes and superstitions that have lasted far beyond their lifespan. Hippocrates's system was so entrenched in the philosophical approach to healing that more than fifteen hundred years later, it was still the leading source of medical knowledge in Western society. Even Shakespeare frequently refers to the four Hippocratic humors in his plays when describing the mental and emotional states of his characters.

Hippocrates believed that these humors created the balance and health of the human body, and when one was out of place, the body would fall to that same imbalance—often in fever, which was represented specifically by an excess of yellow bile. Fever was, in fact, known as a disease that people feared. In the middle ages, it was assumed to be a depiction of demonism incarnate. Heat, like the sun. Fire, something to be feared. Something devilish, something causing harm, illness, death. If this was what was consuming the corpus, why wouldn't it be feared?

The word "fever" comes from the Latin *febris*, "fever," related to *fovere*, "to warm, heat." Fever is also known as pyrexia, from the Greek *pyressein*, "to be feverish, to be ill of fever." This, of course, comes from *pyretos*, "fever, burning heat," related to *pyr*, "fire." The centuries-old Hippocratic prescription for the disease consisted of a new diet or exercise to rebalance those humors and restore health and harmony to the body.

And so fever preyed upon the human race in numerous forms. Typhoid fever. Yellow fever. Q fever. Bilious fever. Scarlet fever. Dengue fever. Valley fever. Crimean-Congo hemorrhagic fever.

It wasn't until the late nineteenth century, when pathophysiology and words like "microbes" and "pyrogens" were tossed around ad hoc following their discovery, that medicine began to evolve beyond the ancient presumption that fever was a fire within the body, a disease to either rebalance or bleed out. Somewhere in the late 1880s, Sir William Osler of Johns Hopkins Medical School and his colleagues discovered that this wasn't exactly true. In a reversal of nearly two thousand years of medical practice, it was determined that fever was not, in fact, the cause of disease, but rather a *sign* of it. A signal to the outside world that there is something wrong in the body.

Yes, as Hippocrates claimed, there was an imbalance, but instead of the fever being the source of the imbalance, it was actually a reflection of it. Fever was the body trying to fight like a million invisible soldiers on the battlefield to stop an infection, a virus, a plague from within. Though it may seem anything but, fever, in an essential way, became our friend: an indicator that something is not right within the body, its defense against infection. What a triumphant allegory. What a reversal of presumption and knowledge. Hippocrates wasn't completely wrong. There *was*, in fact, an imbalance. It was simply that our attack of that imbalance, our need to reconfigure the humors, came from a different place.

THOUGH DOCTORS ADVISE US THAT we'll probably go home soon, our plans quickly change.

Infectious disease specialists are called back.

Let's test for rare diseases. Let's test for diseases that aren't typical in this part of the world, in this time of year.

Neurology is called back.

Perhaps this is just the body's reaction to the reabsorption of blood in the brain.

Neurosurgery is called back.

No, this can't be just a febrile reaction to the reabsorption of the blood in the brain. The fever is too high.

Hematology is called back.

We can test for Factor "x" and Factor "z." It doesn't fit, but what else can we do?

Neonatology is back in the pilot's chair, trying to devise a plan that won't nosedive this plane into the sea. Abby's presumptive open bed is no longer available for another needy infant.

Is this a side effect of multiple antibiotics? Antivirals?

No.

Is it a zebra?

Halfway through any episode of any medical drama on TV,

the zebra always arrives, striped and ready. The departure hugs are always too soon. Healing hasn't yet occurred because it's only thirty minutes in and we're watching an hour-long drama. "This is where it is usually Wegener's," Amir says, referring to a relatively rare autoimmune disease he treats, while watching *House*. "It always returns to rheumatology," he often says with a smile. This time, though, the team invites him to discuss, to offer any suggestions.

"Can we test for Kawasaki's?" Amir asks, knowing full well how unlikely it is. "For vasculitis?"

Two more diseases I've never heard of. Two more diseases that are not even closely on point, one of which is not even rheumatological, but at least there is something to try. A few symptoms match, but not enough. They oblige, kindly. There are no other options, though. They all know it. They've already tested for everything else. Zebras may be all that are left. The more brains in use, the better, because Abby's body is sweltering, the fire within it blazing outward to the skin, and nothing is bringing it down.

The Bake Sale

There is a mystical belief that when at least forty women bake challah, the traditional Jewish bread for Shabbat, with specific prayers for recovery for one person, there is a *segulah*, or a good omen that God will hear them and help. Yael and her rabbi have been in continual communication during Abby's hospitalization, and at his suggestion, she wants to host a challah bake for Abby.

"Invite all your friends," she tells us. "Or give me a list and I'll invite them."

Amir and I have never heard of such a custom, and don't feel comfortable inviting people to my in-laws' home for a mystical, mysterious, religious event of which we know nothing, wherein women who probably don't even know Abby will knead dough for hours in prayer for her recovery.

How bizarre it would be for strangers to be thinking of her. How confusing for us to permit or even encourage people to say prayers in her name when we are not doing the same. Perhaps what concerns me more about the challah bake is the genderization of it all. It is about baking, a stereotypically traditional woman's role. Perhaps if men were permitted to knead dough, too, it might change my perspective; but even then, I'm sure I would still be skeptical.

At first we are inclined to tell her no, but we look at the rabbinical baseball card in Abby's crib and think that we cannot turn down good thoughts, no matter the form they arrive. Friends of all faiths sent their own prayers over the previous days, and I welcome them, even as I refrain from offering my own.

Amir and I call it the Bake Sale.

"Exchange ages and mix in boys, and you've got Rice Krispies treats on the side of a street corner raising money for the band to go to Regionals," we joke.

We attempt humor. It's paltry at best, but we need it.

A few days pass in the timeless existence of in-patient hospital life. The faces of Children's Hospital surround us. The anorexic-looking blond teenager, smothered with freckles and unembarrassed by her IV pole, following her mother eagerly on a Sunday evening to a table in the cafeteria. The adolescent, shrunken by illness, sinking into his oversized clothing and wheelchair, surrounded by at least twenty family members on a Sunday afternoon, to celebrate his birthday? Church? A family event? The Orthodox Jewish family, their children climbing all over the playground outside the cafeteria, *tsit-tsit* hanging on either side.

The new mother crying to her sister on Skype three thousand miles away in New Jersey.

"Did you give Yael a list of people to invite?" I ask Amir in the days leading up to the Bake Sale.

He says no.

"You?"

"No," I say.

I am barely speaking to people. The only person I see daily is Yael, whose visits to the hospital fill me with comfort. I need her here and yet I don't understand this thing she is organizing. I haven't spoken to friends in weeks, save Kendall, who has already experienced something like this. The Bake Sale isn't going to be the first interaction I have with the outside world. It isn't going to be how I speak to new friends in Los Angeles, where I've lived for only a short time. If I don't understand this custom, how could I request others to join in? If I don't believe in it, how could I ask others to take time out of their day to participate? If people want to bake challah on their own, I will welcome that, but it will not be at my request.

I HOLD ABBY IN MY ARMS, trying to reacquaint her with my breast, when my phone buzzes. It's Yael.

"Can you go on Skype?" she asks.

Abby is finally nursing well and I don't want to ruin the latch; it has taken days for her to relearn this basic function, for us to begin to rebond. This, the doctors remind me, is a great sign. She is able to feed, to suck, to swallow. She is also moving all four extremities. She has no facial palsies, no visible droops. I hear these facts frequently mentioned by the doctors, but I do not take them in.

"Sure," I say, opening my computer and shifting the camera to my face. I tell her I don't want to speak with anyone, but I'll be a silent observer. I'm curious, intrigued. Abby continues to nurse.

More than forty women—mostly strangers—are already at my in-laws' home, singing in unison.

Hails of *Shema*, the centerpiece of Jewish prayer that often starts many rituals such as this one, sing at me through the screen. Yael smiles and then carries the computer around so that all these women can say hello. I'm in a movie that is not my own and every way my own, being pitied by people I do not know. But when the music begins, I hear forty strong voices sing together in a powerful sound instantly bringing my body to tears.

Voices of individuals who sing daily or who merely sing once a year join other strangers in a single note as they begin to hum a melody I recognize. The unifying sound of those forty voices rings in my ears. It is the same sound that connects all organs of my body when listening to "Ah Tutti Contenti" at the finale of *The Marriage of Figaro*, in which a company of opera singers comes together in harmony, or hearing the company of *Les Misérables* sing "One Day More" at the end of Act I, a seamless fusion of five sounds in one, or recalling the peace I felt as a child musician in youth symphony when each instrument clashed to tune until settling on that simple A major. Following the violin's lead, woodwinds, brass, tympani, strings, so many souls, so many sounds, so many voices all become one.

My father started teaching me to play the violin when I was four years old. He started learning how to play himself around the same age. I'd always dreamed of teaching my own child at four, too. I went to music camp as a young child. I developed semi-permanent callouses over my fingertips after years of practicing scales and arpeggios and Mozart on the thin black neck of the violin. I fell in love with an opera singer when I was eighteen, and we dated for most of college. He died in a flash flood when I was twenty-nine. I would do almost anything to hear his voice once more, to feel the otherworldly communion when connected to music, to voices.

In Peter Shaffer's Tony- and Academy Award–winning script,

Amadeus, the Italian composer Antonio Salieri connects music to a higher power when he describes the work of his rival, Wolfgang Amadeus Mozart:

> Extraordinary! On the page it looked nothing. The beginning simple, almost comic. Just a pulse—bassoons and basset horns—like a rusty squeezebox. Then suddenly—high above it—an oboe, a single note, hanging there unwavering, till a clarinet took over and sweetened it into a phrase of such delight! This was no composition by a performing monkey! This was a music I'd never heard. Filled with such longing, such unfulfillable longing, it had me trembling. It seemed to me that I was hearing a voice of God.

Though based in a custom unknown to me in a setting that embodies my frustrations with gender-specific events, the music coming from my in-laws' house shifts my balance, and it elevates me. I'm not thinking of the fact that it is women braiding bread; it is people, regardless of gender. I'm not thinking of the fact that these are requests to God, for they are simply voices talking, singing, taking shape in whatever form the listener needs. And when those forty people come together in a home that isn't mine, with voices and faces that I do not recognize, and they settle on a single note, I begin to weep.

I don't know if they see me on the computer screen or if I

want them to see. I don't know if it is the content of the singing, for it is a Hebrew melody I know well despite not speaking the language. With the rotating camera on the other end, face after face after face looks to me, smiles at me, perhaps some even confused at their own presence at this strange ritual. I'm not hearing prayers to God, nor requests for recovery—but rather music. Unifying voices. Bread braided into voices, untrained sopranos, altos, baritones, fueling me.

I don't know if the Bake Sale helps Abby, but I think it helps others discover some way to think they are helping, to be proactive, to take control in their own ways. It's not their words, but the music mixed with the vignettes of faces, the brown eyes, blue eyes, green eyes, shifting, moving on the other end of the computer in a montage of support I need at this moment.

HOURS BEFORE THE BAKE SALE was scheduled to begin, Amir and I sat in the hospital cafeteria, afraid to discuss what was about to transpire at his parents' home. I had lived in the hospital for two weeks. Abby's fever had progressed for the entire second week. We still had no way to explain what Yael was doing. We tried not to laugh. We swore to each other that if Abby's fever broke that night, it would have nothing to do with the anti-feminist Bake Sale taking place at his parents' house in just a few short hours. What's more, it would have absolutely nothing to do with that night's previous medical determination, which informed us that if the fever did not break by morning, the doctors would have to tap her spinal column again with another lumbar puncture. A coincidence in full.

Her fever breaks that night. It is our first upturn of events. Forty-eight hours of monitoring later, we are discharged from the hospital. The acute concern is over. The immediate uncertainty no longer.

We can go home.

Part Two

SUB-ACUTE

UNCERTAINTY

. . .

Sub-acute

Between acute and chronic; denoting the course
of a disease of moderate duration or severity.

—Stedman's Medical Dictionary

Earthquakes

I experienced my first earthquake while taking the California bar exam. In a cavernous room of thousands of future lawyers, half of us ducked under our tables while the other half continued writing, uninterrupted.

"What were you thinking?" I asked a few who continued writing after the earth stopped shaking.

"It's the *bar exam!*" they said. "I'm not fucking around. You only get one shot!"

Of course, you are entitled to as many opportunities to pass the test as you need. What you don't necessarily get is a second chance after part of a building crashes down on you. When the building shook, I mimicked what I'd seen on TV and hid under my table in the conference center with hundreds of other test takers.

Some of them had even brought the test with them. I guess that was supposed to demonstrate a commitment to the law.

My second earthquake is while I am sleeping by Abby's bed during our second week in the NICCU. It is probably one of the safest places I could have been. Confined inside the protected walls of a newly renovated hospital, I wake up to phone calls and texts asking if I am OK. I don't even realize that the earth is shaking beneath us hours earlier. It is one of the first nights I am able to sleep.

Hospitals can offer emotional safety where the outside world often fails. I frequently forget this. I want the comfort of my home; I want to escape the sterile, cold hallways, but I also want the immediate access to help and answers (if they exist) with the push of a button. I want Abby to come home, but I want her to stay in the hospital a little bit longer so that they can monitor her for seizures and stop them immediately if they begin. I want what I know I can't have.

We are discharged with very few instructions. She hasn't seized once since the day we brought her into the hospital. Her fever has broken. She has no visible deficits from the bleed, a positive indication for the future. She is still breathing and sucking and eating, and all four limbs are moving. My family members note how well she looks. Perhaps they are blinded in part by hope, by love, by the prophetic outcome they want, but to me and Amir, she is gaunt and pale, thin and frightened. There is no need to keep her in-patient, though, so home she comes, with no framework in place if this recurs, except to return to the hospital.

While Abby was hospitalized, Amir and I were immersed in the interactive support of trauma: of daily emails and texts, phone calls and messages. Generous offers to visit from friends and family around the country, gifts of food, promises of nightly cooking into the future, unceasing expressions of love and support. We needed every breath of this despite our lack of reciprocation. But after discharge, there is a presumption that everything is fine. The illness has lifted and the injury is contained. The trauma is over, all is well, and Goddamnit if you don't go out and celebrate. What are not always visible are the aftereffects, the emotional costs of the in-betweenness of posthospitalization. It is here where the frustrations Kendall expressed to me surface. Where the desire for positive thinking is thrust upon you before you can wrap your head around reality, and then have to convince people that you are not a pessimist—you are merely going through the day-to-day of caring for a sick infant.

During the initial weeks after we take Abby home, Los Angeles is privy to several more earthquakes, mostly small. We have some damage: a few broken plates; a glass bowl that shatters, sending deep scratches into our floors. And for the first time, we are in sync, the world and I.

UNCERTAINTY TRAVELS IN MANY COSTUMES. For some, it is the question of when death will arrive. For others, whether cancer will strike. When will I meet my life partner or experience that long-awaited moment of professional success? In *Rosencrantz and*

Guildenstern Are Dead, Stoppard focuses on these minor characters of *Hamlet* as they weave in and out of reality, bumping into
the alternative and melodramatic Hamlet in their universal
search for identity. They are waiting. Waiting for the next step,
for an answer to something while they contemplate life and death.
But the parent work, *Hamlet*, is the one that presents the ultimate
question. In his pursuit for the meaning of life, of course Shakespeare writes Hamlet returning to the universality of uncertainty. He doesn't just ask if he should be. He also asks if he
should *not* be. An uncertain future. An uncertain life. *That* is the
question that trails each of us.

I immerse myself in literature and memoirs on grief and loss,
stories of sick children and sick parents, not knowing what my
future might be. I learn over the course of the next few weeks and
months that without knowing what caused the brain bleed, doctors are no better equipped to predict and prevent a future one.
We won't be able to anticipate problems until they appear, or do
not appear. This is quickly becoming a story that has nothing to
do with grief or planning for grief, or treatment to combat an illness, but rather coping with the uncertainty of health in the dense
fog of evolving medicine. Amir can explain terms to me, provide
statistics where a dangerous Google search would lead to panic,
but talking to him does not replace my need for private contemplation. When he walks away, I reach for a book that isn't there. I
don't want to read psychological studies. I want literature, essays
and short stories, memoir and narrative nonfiction that comfort
me as I walk a similar path. Or just as easily stray from it.

The only way I could make sense of anything was to pull out a notepad inside my tiny room in the NICCU and write. I wrote about what happened, about what might happen, what might not happen. Every night, in between pumping and feedings, scheduled infusions and timed temperature checks, I pulled down the cushions of the couch, covered it with a sheet, lay on my back, and wrote down my questions for the doctors, my thoughts, my fears.

I freely admit that there are far worse cases of illness, injury, and disease. In fact, I can recall several cases on the NICCU floor during our time there alone. These stories—of acute injury and chronic illness, painful decisions with unknowable outcomes, all swarming the spectrum of what makes life uncertain—haunt me. On the hospital floor, I witnessed codes with sadder endings. Babies born prematurely without organs who I suspected would not live beyond the next few days. Children suffering from terminal illnesses. Young children walking in and out of the pediatric intensive care unit fully aware of their medical status. I spoke with some of these parents and just observed others, wondering how they analyzed their future, how they interacted with the outside world, how they explained to their families not only the medical terminology but also the concept of their own uncertain future. For most of them, this is the most difficult part of their stay. Many patients can put on a strong face and bear the pain if they know the outcome. Many parents can prepare, devastatingly so, for home care if they are given specific instructions, which sometimes, though rarely, comes. But without that knowledge and direction, the virus of uncertainty spreads to epidemic proportions.

Time Will Tell

Before we are formally discharged, we wait patiently through the final exit visits from various specialists. I hug our neonatologist and wish her well. I hug our nurses. I wait for the neurosurgeon, whom I know I'll see in a few weeks' time for a follow-up MRI. Above all, I am eager to speak to the neurologist. In my mind, she will be able to at least examine Abby and provide a stencil of clarity that could help me redesign our future.

"What sort of deficits are we looking at?" I ask.

The neurologist shrugs and makes a comment about infant brains being plastic and this being a good thing. But I press her further. Is this simply going to be a bad memory for me, or a different future for her? For all of us?

I hear that plastic brain comment again. The neurologist doesn't smile much. She has a team of students and fellows with her. She seems unimpressed with Abby. She taps on Abby's knees and feet, seeking reflexes. Abby is moving normally. Clearly, the neurologist isn't yet ready to enter the equation and provide a forecast.

"Time will tell," is all I remember her saying before walking out of the room with her team.

Other doctors come and go, signing off on her in-patient care. Most of them do not even require an outpatient follow-up.

"Go home and enjoy your daughter," other doctors say. There's nothing to do right now but wait and watch for hydrocephalus.

Hydrocephalus literally means "water on the brain" and is a build-up of fluid that puts pressure on the brain to swell, causing it to press against the skull. Hydrocephalus, or "hydro" for short, often follows a bleed like Abby's and becomes something that doctors will monitor in Abby over the next few years. It can resolve on its own or resolve with surgical intervention.

We monitor Abby from home with head measurements to see if her head is growing, expanding like a beach ball filling with air ever so slightly. Every few weeks she'll undergo a CT scan to measure the size of the brain ventricles and see if they are growing, potentially causing hydrocephalus. Every few months, we'll get a better image of possible growth with an MRI. If the brain is expanding, then surgery is the next step, which would mean a placement of a shunt, a narrow tubing that could be surgically inserted in order to allow the excess fluid to drain. A dangerous procedure, as anything can be on the brain, that requires cutting into bone and tissue that can change physical and mental abilities with a slight twitch of the hand. Another possibility is an experimental surgery also designed to release the pressure and return the head to normal measurements, and hopefully a normal life. Or perhaps nothing may happen and the blood will continue to reabsorb, there will be no hydrocephalus, and all will be well.

This stage is waiting to watch the grass grow, to see the ticks of the clock shift. It is the natural extension of a brain bleed, a cruel reminder that once you're discharged from the hospital, it's only partially over. Next comes the hydrocephalus scare, and after that, rehabilitation and observation. One neurosurgeon tells us it might be two years until we're out of the woods, while another thinks there will be resolution "one way or another" within the year. Not the cliché that time will heal all wounds, because it may for some and may not for others, but rather the prescription of time as the only source of answers.

During my efforts to learn all I can about hydrocephalus, I read that National Book Award–winning author Sherman Alexie was born with hydrocephalus in the mid-1960s, at a time when brain shunts were being heavily developed. He underwent surgery and had a temporary shunt placed. As one of our most renowned contemporary writers, he serves as a tremendous success story for some hydrocephalic babies and an example of what can happen with surgery, luck, effective therapy, and a superlative canvas.

His early 1990 poem, "Learning to Drown," exemplifies the early trauma of hydrocephalus. In it, he explores how water on the brain is not just a fear from Alexie's mother that the brain will float, but that her son would be trapped and taken from her.

1.

I used to go with my big brother
To a place on the Spokane River
Where he and his friends dared
Each other to swim
All the way across
To the opposite shore.
I would watch them,

Some too scared to swim
Past the shallow
Water, most making it halfway
And coming back, coughing
Water, a few struggling
In the middle
Of the river, treading
Water, my brother
Swimming beyond sight.
I remember watching
Water. I remember
Waiting for my brother,
Wanting to follow him
And recover myself again.

2.

Water on the brain
Makes the definition easier
To understand, anticipates
The questions always asked:
"What kind of dreams did you have?"
"Was it like drowning?"
I can still see my reflection
In water, my face
Flooding the banks, a body

Of water erasing boundaries,
Changing the distance
Between past and present.

3.

I remember the reservation girl
With Down Syndrome,
Weighing over 300 pounds,
Wading in Benjamin Lake,
Feet tangled in weeds,
Falling facedown
Into six inches of water.
My cousin, ten years old,
Trying to lift her,
Trying to turn her over
Trying anything
To make her breathe.

4.

My mother tells me
The doctors would not believe
My skull was growing,
Swelling, until my cousin
Dropped me from a swing.
My mother tells me

I measured
The size of your head every day.
It grew an inch in one week.
But the doctors said no,
It was a mother's imagination
Growing. I had nightmares
You were pressed against walls
Of our house, breaking through,
That it would ever stop.

5.

Driving all night, I hear a story
On the radio about prisoners
Of war in some foreign country.
Their captors had no room left
To house them, nearly 600 men,
So they marched them down
To a nearby river
And drowned all of them,
One by one, while the other
Prisoners watched
From the river bank, silent,
Bowed into themselves.

"Pressed against walls," a fear that you will never stop
drowning. A terror that whatever this is will prevent you from

reaching your potential. An overwhelming emotion independent of and completely relevant to any medical crisis.

Yet there is a glimmer of hope at such a young age. When there is a bleed in the ventricles of the brain, blood has a place to swim; it has a watering hole where it can rest and drain without instantly causing permanent damage. Moreover, in infants the skull is not yet fused together, so when blood collects in the ventricles, expanding them, it has a pressure valve, causing a bulge out of the fontanelle. In an adult where there is no opening in the skull, the blood pushes down on the brain stem potentially causing death.

Think of the spinal column as plumbing. Water from the top flows down to the rest of the pipes, but when the source is blocked, nothing can flow. When hair blocks a shower drain, water cannot leave the tub into the drainage pipes below, so it just continues filling the tub with water and overflows. For example, an adult brain is a tub with a hard lid on top. When the water overflows due to the blocked drain, there is nowhere for it to go. In an infant, though, the tub is covered with a handful of soft clay plates not yet hardened into cement. If the drain is clogged on an infant tub and the water cannot overflow, we can see the soft clay plates shifting and expanding to contain the water, buying time to unclog the drain.

Every hour I hear whispers behind the poetry.

Go back to your normal life. Enjoy your baby.

Does that mean I should enjoy her because I won't have much time left? Or I should enjoy her as if this didn't happen? As if it's not going to happen again. Or get worse. Or until her full head of hair needs to be shaved to create a clean palate for a scalpel. I close my eyes and see my ten-year-old self's eyes observing a workbench for a surgeon, and the goosebumps rise on my forearms.

Before we leave the hospital, a physical therapist swings by our room and is the only one who provides us with a plan. A silly computer printout of stretches and exercises. The gift of phantom control. If we do these, the neurons in her brain may reconnect properly and this will be a bad memory alone. Physical therapy in the form of "early intervention" may be the best solution. One of a few ways to take control back and intervene.

I take the printouts. They are nothing more than regular infant exercises that we do anyway. Moving her legs in circles. Shifting them back and forth. Ensuring a specific amount of time that she's placed on the belly so that the neck strengthens and the two sides of the body are forced to use muscles evenly. I don't know how yoga moves and massages on a newborn can fix something this big.

And still they don't know what happened. The neonatologist spent many nights with us, admitting she didn't know what had happened. She spent all night researching and thinking about Abby, she told us. I respected her for that honesty. She then asked Amir back into the doctor's lounge to discuss the case, asking for any thoughts he had on it because, quite simply, they were stumped.

Yet Abby is discharged without her team figuring out what happened, without knowing if seizures would recur, without knowing if she'd be put on a path to, what medicine would deem, normalcy. The range of options: slight physical delays that could be remedied in a year or two with physical therapy on one end, or severe developmental deficits. A completely normal future or a re-envisioned normal. A or Z or anything in between.

But go home and enjoy your daughter.

I obsess over statistics I find online about Grade IV brain bleeds, the most perilous form of a brain hemorrhage. Some sites claim a 20 percent chance of mortality and 90 percent chance of severe neurological damage without painting a specific picture. Will we be aiding our adult child in her daily routine or will this be her college application essay topic? *This is our daughter,* we say to each other. *We love her and will be here for her regardless.* But now, maybe we shouldn't have a second child. We always wanted two, but perhaps not anymore. Abby may need all our help, all our attention. Or she may not. Maybe she'll be a genius and none of this will matter. Maybe she'll be like my brother—profoundly sick as an infant, in and out of hospitals for years with severe respiratory problems, and later a college athlete.

But forget the long-term neurological concerns: the focus is now on hydrocephalus and neurosurgery. How can I monitor for this at home? I don't have the tools, the skills, the education. How will I know if that rolling eye jitter is normal, or if she is crying because of cerebrospinal fluid leaking into her brain tissue, blocking flow into the spinal column, debilitating her in the same way it did Amir, who could describe the pain after the roller coaster? Is she just acting like a baby and crying for hunger? Or is it just gas? Is that twitch in her hand just fussiness or is it another seizure? Was she pulling her own hair so ferociously before the bleed or is she simply figuring out how to grab? Is she exploring the way her tongue moves within her mouth, or are sensory issues starting to form?

From home, we must monitor for seizure activity. We must measure the size of her head and visit our pediatrician monthly for official head measurements. Abby must have a cranial ultrasound every other week so the doctors can evaluate the size of the ventricles and measure them against each other, to determine if they are expanding from the blood spilled inside.

The doctors listen to me as I raise the same questions at each visit. To feel marginalized for your uncertainty while *learning to drown* is an unfair and unfathomable position, particularly when it is one of the few universal experiences we share.

But if the head measurements increase, she may have hydrocephalus. She may need brain surgery. I'll have to understand how a shunt works and follow the path of replacement every so many years, if necessary, learning where it drains, and all the risks carried with neurosurgery on an infant.

First, though, let's just wait and see.

Go home and enjoy your daughter.

But if she's inconsolable, it could be hydrocephalus.

If she's seizing, it could be hydrocephalus.

If there is fever and vomiting, it could be hydrocephalus.

If the soft spot in the head, the fontanelle, is bulging, it could be hydrocephalus.

Watch for it.

Wait for it.

Feel it from time to time to make sure it is still soft to the touch.

Go home and enjoy your daughter.

I go home and google "uncertainty is." The search reveals the following answers in the top three: (1) "uncertainty is the essence of romance"; (2) "uncertainty is killing me"; (3) "uncertainty is the gateway to possibility."

A positive choice. A negative choice. A hopeful one.

Waiting for Godot

In January 1953 in Paris, the French playwright Samuel Beckett debuted his play *Waiting for Godot*, a tragicomedy in two acts. Although critics have dissected its theme through the lenses of Freudian and Jungian psychology, post–World War II politics, Christianity, and existential philosophy, the play has always been, to my mind, most profound in its treatment of uncertainty. The two central characters, Vladimir and Estragon, of unknown age and background, foolish in many ways, sit around a tree on an empty stage waiting for someone by the name of Godot to arrive.

American scholars make much of the title and its religious undertones. Are Vladimir and Estragon waiting for a God that will never come? Beckett has stated that Godot does not mean "God"; in fact, he wrote the play in French, where "Godot" translates as "boot," and "God" as "Dieu." Translations aside, it seems unlikely that he wouldn't have anticipated such interpretations, particularly since he translated his own work into English.

Beckett scholar Lois Gordon wrote in her book *Reading Godot* that "his poetry may have been unspeakably beautiful, but it stood as a testimony of human industry in the face of terror." Indeed, uncertainty may exist in "the face of terror" because so much of it is often confused with the unknown. Though they do overlap, they are not always the same. Uncertainty is a fork in a river, while the unknown is the open sea. Uncertainty is a sliver of knowledge, while the unknown may be blissful ignorance. Knowing a hint of information can cause the terror of uncertainty to swell. Like the drop of blood in a Hitchcock film, the *hint* of gore is much more terrifying than a bucket of red paint (or no paint at all). It is the possibilities that creep into one's subconscious, the glances of injury and illness that make us fear it. The "face of terror" is the reminder that we have seen just a little bit, but not everything. It is a plane crashing over the Indian Ocean without an explanation. It is the arbitrary selection of inherited disease. Of cancer. And unlike a heart attack—which, while horrifying, may be predicated by hardened arteries, heart disease, poor nutrition, or genetic predisposition—a brain hemorrhage on a healthy six-week-old has almost no clear etiology. It is this unknown source that leads to uncertainty and fear. Fear keeps us stoic in our countenance as if our feet are caught hardened in cement where the incident took place, immobilizing us.

By the end of the play, Vladimir realizes that movement is essential to destroy monotony and fear. "Astride of a grave and a difficult birth," he says. "Down in the hole, lingeringly, the grave-digger puts on the forceps. We have time to grow old. The air is full of our cries. But habit is a great deadener."

While waiting for answers, particularly answers that may never come or may come outside of our control, I have one foot in the grave and one in infancy, and if I continue in stagnation, if I continue in the "great deadener" of habit, I will lose time and lose much of myself. This is the struggle of hospitalization—stagnation and terror of waiting following discharge. Time is still as I wait for answers, but when I don't know when those answers will come, I know that I cannot be stuck with one foot in the grave because that one foot will ground my entire body.

Sunsets

For weeks following Abby's discharge, she stares ahead from time to time with a look of surprise. Her sclera, the whites of her eyes, covers nearly half of the opening of the eye socket on the top, while the bottom third comprises her iris, her pupil. Her irises are sitting so far down into her eye sockets that it seems as though a string is pulling them to her chin. She looks terrified and aware of her terror, bringing me back to Poe's endlessly dark forest.

I want to take a photo of her expression for documentation but don't want the flash accidentally going off, potentially causing another seizure. Maybe it is my constant photography that has caused all of this. I consider selling my camera equipment, giving up photography as a hobby. I tell her pediatrician about it, but she isn't concerned, because Abby looks great on each of her visits. The white-eyed gaze returns only when she is placed in a more upright position like a car seat or a stroller.

I call my brother, who has been taking photos of her every time he sees her.

"Did you notice that weird eye thing today?" I ask him. He had just left my apartment to go home. "I could have sworn I saw you pushing her in the stroller and she was doing that weird eye thing while you were taking photos of her."

I realize after I say this that I sound accusatory. I feel bad yet I don't at all. I can't own either sentiment. I want to accuse him yet I know he's done nothing wrong.

"I'm sorry," I quickly say to him. "I didn't mean that you caused the weird eye thing. You know what I'm talking about. I just want evidence. I want to send a picture to Patricia."

Patricia is my sister's best friend from medical school and also, conveniently, a pediatric neurologist in New York. The gracious recipient of phone calls, pictures, and texts at all hours of the night for weeks, Patricia has become my savior, my own friend. I am acutely aware of this position of privilege, and I am endlessly grateful.

"Sasha?" I say, feeling the need to fill the space with words. I always feel the need to fill the space with words. "I keep describing *the look*, but nobody knows what I'm talking about," I tell him.

I think I'm failing to properly describe it. He takes too long to respond to me.

"Oh," he finally says. "I'm so sorry."

"What?"

"I deleted those," he says. "I didn't want to look at them. I didn't want to have them in my phone."

I don't reply. Abby looks back at me without the look.

A few hours later, as I stroll Abby around the neighborhood, her irises set downward like the sun, leaving a tremendous sky of whiteness for me to see. A vast atmosphere where anything could happen. Her eyes momentarily freeze in that position, and I take a photo. Five minutes later, I'm on the phone with Patricia, who tells me that they *could be* what is called "sunset eyes," a symptom of hydrocephalus in infants. Though Abby's do not fully present with such severity, she tells me that I should probably speak with her neurosurgeon about it.

A sun rising is an image of beauty. Oranges, crisp yellows, dark reds, sloshing together in a warm autumn palette. I know the scene well. I know its partner scene, too. The descending sun with a darker selection of cobalt blue and purple, charcoal gray. Every day I can count on it. It is and should be a symbol of movement, growth. What is noticeably stunning about a sunset is the arch of the star itself. The round sun partially hidden, half in slumber, half awake, until being put to sleep by the moon. A sunset lives a half-life; or, rather, it divides its time between day and night, lightness and darkness, life and death. A life cut short. The day turning to night, a sun hiding behind a hillside, a star losing its power, saying good-bye. Ending. A time-honored tradition of reliability, comfort, and now concern.

I thank Patricia for providing me with language. After all, language is what most people lack in medical crises. We become mute, unable to communicate without the proper vocabulary to express fact, detail, physical summaries. Having words with which to engage empowers me, despite the fact that it changes nothing in reality. I thank her for her willingness to speak with me with a kindness I wish most doctors have.

Days at the Salon

Abby and I visit the hospital every other week for cranial ultra-sounds. In those dark rooms, she falls asleep nursing on my breast so that she is calm and still as the ultrasound technicians place warm gel on a soothing probe and massage the top of her head. We lie together for more minutes in silence while the technician finishes taking the images. We do this until six weeks have passed and it is time for her to go in for an MRI, where the images will be stronger and she'll be seen by a neurosurgeon.

Because she is so young and her skull is not yet fully formed, we are lucky to have the opportunity to glance into the brain with an ultrasound probe. We are able to see beneath the skull because the fontanelle provides a temporary window into the brain. Fast forward a year and this would not be possible. The fontanelle closes by twelve to fifteen months. Another reason we should have answers within the next year or two—a short period in retrospect, but interminable in the moment.

Every other week, I reassure the ultrasound technicians that we know about the abnormalities they are finding with their gel-filled probes. Every other week, I watch with accepting eyes as the technicians taking images of Abby freeze before the screen, trying to mask their surprise of facts I already know. They don't have Abby's full medical history in the computer because we are at a different hospital, one that accepts our insurance. Every other week, I drive to the hospital for the cranial ultrasounds, and I slip into three new garments: parent, self-regulator, regulator of others.

I calm Abby as she breastfeeds still so that the ultrasound images can be taken with clarity.

I calm myself when I see the reaction of the ultrasound technicians to the images, knowing that they are seeing this for the first time. I know nothing new has happened, and yet I don't. The two-headed beast leading me astray once again, my head and heart misdirecting each other.

I calm the ultrasound technicians, informing them that, yes, oh yes, we are on top of this thing. You don't need to send us back to the emergency room right now. We know all about it. That's why we're here.

I call these visits our Days at the Salon. For the hours following the ultrasounds, Abby's curls wind tightly on the top of her head like a rooster's comb, and even she finds it funny. We create new hairstyles for hours afterward, playing with the ultrasound gel until six weeks pass and the first real glimpse into the future arrives.

Anesthesia

I've read other writers describe watching their children befall
the mask of anesthesia. Life and then nothing. Consciousness and
then its opposing force. In *On Immunity*, Eula Biss describes this
disturbing performance as "a rehearsal of death."

Seven weeks following discharge, we walk into a new hospital
and sign forms again, carrying Abby into forced slumber. This
time she is lucky to escape intubation and succumbs to only general anesthesia. No understanding of her own risks. The responsibility of making medical decisions for another person is a feeling
that cannot be summarized into the single word, "responsibility."
It is at once a privilege, a matter of unnerving and unconditional
love. I don't know if Abby will be intubated again this time. I
don't know if the bleeding has stopped, no matter what the ultra-
sounds show. She's not yet fully vaccinated. She's too young, and
her immunizations have been delayed several weeks because of
her hospitalization. Airborne diseases glitter the hallways of the
hospital in invisible design. I cover Abby with a breathable blanket. Amir holds her far away from the other patients.

"Only one parent can go in," the nurses say as we carry Abby
into the MRI room. Amir and I take turns, each invited into the
process for just a brief moment.

I hold Abby and she smiles at me. She also smiles at the anesthesiologist. Her smiles are infectious and indiscriminating.

ELIZABETH L. SILVER

"She'll just look like she's sleeping," he tells me.

It happens swiftly. There is no counting backward with an infant, so instead it's just a little nursery rhyme singing her to sleep. Her immobility does not terrify me. It only makes me sad.

"All right, it's done," the anesthesiologist says to me.

"That's it?"

"Pretty quick," he says, rather proudly. "I'll be here the whole time monitoring things, but it looks good. We'll start now."

I take that as my cue and begin to walk away until he stops me.

"You can say something to her," he says.

I don't understand. I had said "I love you" to her a million times that morning, but now I say it aloud into her ear as if this is the one that counts because they can hear it. It feels forced and awkward.

Minutes later, I sit in the waiting room. The information monitor tells me that x-rays were only thus named because scientists did not know the kind of radiation used to achieve the effect. "X" was meant to indicate the unknown. The name stuck.

I'm skeptical, so I look it up. In 1895 German scientist Wilhelm Conrad Röntgen discovered x-rays by accident while experimenting with a cathode ray tube and his wife's hand. He realized that this particular type of ray would pass through human tissue, leaving metal (his wife's wedding ring) and bone to be seen. Now we know that x-rays are electromagnetic radiation, but it's easier to just call them "X." It makes sense to rely on the known unknowns. It gives a sense of tradition, comfort.

People seem to be comfortable with what we don't know so long as it works. It's often the moment something stops working that we question its source, its capability, its worth, and want to know why.

I say, *I love you, Abby*, quietly to myself every minute, my own form of silent prayer to Röntgen, to the anesthesiologist, to nothing and no one in particular, until we are called back, and she comes out of anesthesia successfully.

Waiting Rooms

I'm in the waiting room of the first neurosurgeon's office about to find out the results from Abby's first outpatient MRI. Well–decorated artwork stretched from floor to ceiling. We get free water with the logo of the office printed on the bottles.

It is hours after Abby has awakened from anesthesia. She is cranky but not terribly so. I wait for an extra hour. It's OK. These are *neurosurgeons. Pediatric* neurosurgeons. Nothing I do will ever be as important—not in writing or in law. I wonder if other doctors feel impotent comparatively. Still, I know that this pediatric neurosurgeon is just a person. He is not a God. He's a meticulously well-trained technician, and yet I wait for his answers the way a penitent stands outside a confessional hoping for absolution.

While I wait, the termites of guilt return. Hospitals are infested with them, as are waiting rooms.

We are called into his office and he tells us it doesn't look good. He tells us that the ventricles have, indeed, expanded. It is mild, but still.

. . . still . . .

. . . but still . . . what?

My body hurts.

The tips of my fingernails.

The hair follicles on my scalp.

The pain around my cesarean incision, nearly healed, travels through my abdomen to my chest.

The neurosurgeon keeps talking, speaking about the images on the oversized screen on the wall where Abby's scans are displayed.

"At least the fontanelle is soft and her head is measuring on the large end of normal," he says. "It's still within normal limits, but at the high end."

Amir's head is on the large end of normal. It's his joke with his childhood friends. He has a big head. Maybe it's just genetic and not hydrocephalus.

But the neurosurgeon discusses the possibilities for surgery. There are options and choices, though he does not provide them. Not yet, he says. Not until we need them.

She'll probably need a shunt, but "I'll give her just one more chance," he says. "We'll run another MRI in three months." By then, he suspects, hydrocephalus will develop to a point that his hands will be tied. "My hands will be tied," he says, deadpan, pantomiming handcuffs with a scalpel between his fingers.

A WEEK LATER WE VISIT a second neurosurgeon. I can't tell the difference anymore between a minute and a week. I can only see my daughter smile and roll over and nurse and giggle. There is nothing noticeably abnormal at all. That's got to be a sign.

It has been two months since our discharge from the NICCU, and I am still living in this sub-acute uncertainty, the space between. This appointment is for a second opinion, but truly it's a first. This is the doctor who observed and treated Abby while she was hospitalized. The office is not fancy. It is academic. I trust this person. There is no logical basis for this trust, but I allow it to guide me.

I look around the waiting room and my heart stutters. Disney movies play on the TV. A small child's table is placed before it. On the faces waiting beside me are sunset eyes and enlarged craniums. Brains floating in water. Hydrocephalus. I see buoyant eyes that no longer see the world through the prism of innocence. I see parents who are tired, exhausted, frustrated, fed up. Mothers who feel pregnant far beyond delivery. Fathers who are equally lost. Parents who look to their children, the television, the fish tank, and the ceiling in that order, over and over again. I am in the same place as these parents. We are here for the same reasons. Some of us may need a shunt placed, some may not. But we are all waiting together, refusing to speak to one another.

Moments later, I am waiting inside the examining room. It is beautiful outside. We are behind a large glass window, overlooking the Hollywood sign and the hills. Buildings speckle the landscape as colorful confetti. Inverse favelas. One neurosurgeon's office perfumed with money, while the other with certificates. This one has seen Abby since day one, though, visited her in the hospital every day. This is the doctor who is well acquainted with her acute trauma and the uncertainty ailing us, who's been following us as we monitor and test for hydrocephalus.

"Let's repeat the MRI in another three months," he says, agreeing with the first neurosurgeon, but less inclined to jump to surgery. He doesn't think she'll need a shunt and mentions nothing about his hands being tied, but does want to see what the scan shows again in three months before making decisions.

So we wait.

Statistics

I review those same statistics that dictate affiliations with injuries like this one. I lie in bed comatose. I stop washing my hair, my teeth. I nurse. I contemplate returning to full time legal work, despite my life's goal of working as a writer, because there is more of a structured routine to it. I don't know what maternity leave means to a writer. I'm trying to get back to a professional life. It's been four months. I need work to put me into a semblance of routine. I reread the 20 percent chance mortality statistic on-line. I reread the 90 percent neurological damages statistic. They tell me words I understand intellectually. They inform me of what may happen because of this injury. I try to ignore statistics and learn what it means to go home and enjoy my baby. I hate that line. A dictate of emotion, futility embraced.

Fast and Slow

Daniel Kahneman is the 2002 winner of the Nobel Prize in Economic Sciences. Kahneman, a research psychologist and professor, worked extensively in the field of decision making in the face of uncertainty. Kahneman concluded that our minds are divided into two selves: System 1, which is "Fast Thinking" and System 2, which is "Slow Thinking." Each system does its own work in helping us make decisions. System 1 is fast: our instinct, our intuition, our impulsive behavior, the things we say and do automatically. System 2 is in charge of self-control: it is slow, deliberate, and conscious.

Kahneman writes in his bestselling book *Thinking Fast and Slow* that "the conclusion is straightforward: self-control requires attention and effort. . . . One of the main functions of System 2 is to monitor and control thoughts and actions 'suggested' by System 1, allowing some to be expressed directly in behavior and suppressing or modifying others."

It's interesting to consider Kahneman's two-system theory in the context of medical decision making. In the acute period of uncertainty, I had to think fast. Though I wasn't consciously thinking about my actions, I still made decisions on instinct. I took videos. I consulted friends who may have more knowledge on the subject than me. I drove to the best ER for children that I could. I didn't think about these decisions—I just followed my impulse to do whatever I could to help my daughter. That must have been my System 1 thinking in place: fast, impulsive, reactive. It may also have been my System 1 thinking regulated by years of System 2 analysis structuring how my System 1 fast thinking might materialize.

Once we arrived at the ER and were pulled back, it was less about my thinking and more about the doctors and nurses who had to think fast and rely on their instincts and training to make the right decisions. I wasn't given many options at that point. I was not provided a list of decisions, each choice carrying separate consequences that could be weighed against the others. When my daughter was having a seizure, my System 1 made the fast-thinking decision to rush to a children's ER to be seen immediately.

But that time is now over. I'm not thinking fast anymore. I am no longer running to the emergency room with a newborn, desperate for a quick fix. I'm thinking slowly. Slow-motion slowly. I'm waiting for things to develop or not to develop. I'm waiting for months to pass so that tests can be administered to monitor progress. I am waiting and watching for Abby to eventually hit milestones. It is slow. Dreadfully slow. And in this time I think, I analyze, I rethink moments and decisions made in the past and those I must make in the future with that System 2 mind. I fear derailment. I fear it daily whenever I watch her sleep, when I see her hiccup, when I see her rub her eyes, and when I hear her cry. I'm watching her grow, enjoying it and fearing it all the same. I'm waiting for results in between those tests, and, finally, I am given decisions to make.

In between each MRI and each appointment, I research Pediatric Neurosurgeon One at one institution. I research Pediatric Neurosurgeon Two at another institution. Both are stellar, sure. Both are exceptional minds and leaders in their field. But how do I choose which one to trust if surgery is required? And how do I decide what kind of surgery?

Let's just wait and repeat this again in three months, I hear over and over again.

And in those three months between each MRI, I revisit these questions equally, testing one neurosurgeon's opinion against another's, one surgical option against another, trying to decide my daughter's fate on logical conclusions. Or perhaps merely chance. Why do I trust one more than another? Why does anyone? Every three months when Abby is admitted to the hospital for an MRI, Amir and I must decide whether to listen to one over the other, as each three-month scan results in a new opinion, a new decision to be made at that time: surgery or not. If both agree, then we are comfortable. In doing so, we must be relying on System 2, which Kahneman says "is capable of reasoning, and it is cautious." And if there is disagreement, we will get a third opinion until there is a comfortable consensus.

"You experience greater cognitive ease in perceiving a word you have seen earlier and it is this sense of ease that gives you the impression of familiarity," writes Kahneman, pushing the analysis of these two systems further. The same I suspect is true in terms of relying on doctors. Though both are exceptional physicians, I'm so much more comfortable with the first neurosurgeon I see—not because he told me what I wanted to hear, but because he was the first doctor I relied upon in my time of crisis. I was familiar with him. The inherent trust was established because he was with me during my daughter's acute medical crisis. This is apparently called the mere exposure effect, a phenomenon in which people develop a preference for things that are more familiar to them. It is instinct and intuition.

I don't care what it's called. I just feel trust.

It is not necessarily an irrational trust, though, but a gut instinct, created from an aggregate sensory life. Perhaps this is the two systems working together in this decision-making process. From experience, from years crafting my writing, from the practice of law, from years of studying people, from living near doctors, from carrying a child. There is a reason physicians become better with time. Experience helps their analysis with a mixture of concrete diagnostic help. The gut instinct helps the rest of the decision making, the action, the practice. This is clearly true for any profession, any identity. The same is true in patients when given time and knowledge with which to make a decision.

Days after the two neurosurgery visits, I wait in another pediatric neurologist's office. It is old and carries remnants of a different era of medicine. This doctor still takes her notes by hand. Behind her is a library of textbooks that must be out of date, and on the top of the bookshelves sits a collection of large wooden hourglasses.

I speak with the neurologist about possible prognoses for Abby. Her comments are neither negative nor positive. They are empty, without definition, without guidance. All she can state is what happened in the past. Her words are nothing I haven't heard or worried about or googled or researched or discussed with other doctors before this visit, but she speaks to me—at me—as if I'm a trembling child, hearing this lack of clarity for the first time. I've heard it before. She tells me nothing about Abby's future, apart from recommending physical and occupational therapy. She can't see into the future. Nobody can.

I motion to the hourglasses behind her.

"Are those to indicate the tincture of time?" I ask. "That in neurology, our answers will come pretty much with time. We just have to wait for them."

She laughs, raising an eyebrow in concert.

"No, those are for the kids to play with while I speak with their parents."

I picture that phrase, "the tincture of time," mummified in the past. A phrase recycled from that bygone era of medicine, where house visits populated the streets with aging doctors wearing white caps and carrying oblong leather bags. I envision old extracts, potions, and tinctures bottled into flasks and re-branded as remedies, traveling with old medicine men on long dusty roads to unnamed towns. A prescription of sand slipping through an hourglass. Time is all it will take to heal or find answers. Time and its tincture.

Faith

A friend of mine who is a scholar of Jewish history once said to me, "Doesn't religion give people the *illusion* of certainty? Some sort of stabilizing framework?" Certainly it does. It can help individuals when no answers exist otherwise. It may be precisely that, though—an illusion. Yet does the lack of reality matter? If the illusion is helping someone cope, then it is real.

Religion is a type of faith—belief without concrete knowledge. It represents ideals and codes, guides for life. There is no mathematical law clearly presenting universal truths that one can accept with one hundred percent authority and certainty. Instead, religion offers its own heuristic that people can accept with one hundred percent faith. After all, faith—religion, specifically—is a collection of interpretations, which is why it is so exquisitely rife with conflict. Religion can be seen as the source of the greatest unknown. Yet it is the escape hole so many people visit while watching the "rehearsal of death," or while waiting for test results, or when hoping for healing in a hospital. They pray. Friends send their "thoughts and prayers" in letters and messages and phone calls. Those suffering look up to a proverbial heaven, and often make deals with God.

God only gives you what you can handle, hears the patient or parent dealing with one medical ailment too many. For some, this phrase is arsenic, and for others, a guiding force.

Sophie is a colleague of one of my relatives. Following fertility struggles, she eventually became pregnant, and during her nineteen-week ultrasound, the doctors found a few abnormalities so extreme that they recommended termination. Deeply religious in the Christian faith, Sophie refused, and in time many of those problems resolved in utero. By the following ultrasound, Sophie felt that she was experiencing a miracle. "I knew God would intervene and heal these last issues soon," she said.

Her son, Jay, was born one month premature. His kidneys began to fail, and he was placed on dialysis for eleven hours a day. At fifteen months, he became eligible for a kidney transplant, which Sophie's husband provided. So far, Jay is doing well. He still has problems with his bladder, and eventually, in ten or fifteen years' time, the transplanted kidney from his father will likely fail, at which point he will receive his mother's extra kidney, provided the same health parameters from today remain in place.

I told Sophie about the Bake Sale and my fear of placing too much reliance on prayers to God. What if the outcome was not positive? What would that say about the quality of prayer? Of the person praying? Of God?

"God wouldn't bring this child into the world if he didn't think he'd be fine," she told me, without pause. She didn't need to address my concerns because, despite acknowledging that they exist, she didn't share them. Sophie was raised in a religious environment. Her grandmother is the caretaker of a church. Her community knew what she was experiencing and prayed for her family, prayed for Jay. Religion was her comfort, her way of doing something.

Though "doctors are speculating," she said to me, "God knows everything. He knew my child before he was born. If there's a question about his health, why wouldn't I ask the person who knows him best? . . . I know he has the answer."

Sophie operates without doubt. An absolute belief in something intangible, something that to me feels unknown, unprovable, but to her is fully known with unwavering certainty.

Still, given my experience with the Bake Sale and after so many kind people sent their prayers my way, I was apprehensive to pray in case things did not materialize positively following prayer. For someone with a greater seal on faith, I wanted to know if hers would change if all those prayers did not work in her favor. If tragically the outcome had been different. If—

"If the worst happened," she said, completing my words. "Then God thinks I can do more, handle more."

In an instant, a comfort and ease overtook her. Her face softened, and she smiled. She didn't question her faith. She didn't look elsewhere. She was at peace, in a place of comfort and security in her faith, even if I did not see answers in the same place. It helped her—it helps her—which is all that matters.

This is not to say that either of our beliefs is completely irrational or rational; rather, that my constitution is simply not aligned with hers, or with that of others who rely on faith so passionately to help them cope with the uncertainties in life, medical or otherwise.

I speak with a rabbi about Sophie and the Bake Sale and the Jewish perspective. In response, he asks, "What happens when you drop a computer on a floor?"

I smile. Of course a rabbi would answer a question with a question.

"You cry," I say. I'm a writer.

He laughs. "After you finish crying. What do you do? You press restart, don't you?"

I nod, yes.

You are going to the source for help, he explains.

"The same is true for a child. A young child raised by omnipotent, beneficent parents, when dropped on the floor, rushes to his or her mom or dad, and wants comfort, help, support."

That is the instinct, I say to him.

Parents are the restart button he is discussing. When adults press the restart button after a traumatic event, though, they often look to the only all-knowing type of parent that may be available—God. People project onto *our parent who art in heaven,* he tells me, echoing the well-known prayer to prove a point.

"We want to believe that there is a God driving the universe," he says. "We want to know that there is no accident. No uncertainty. Maybe there is uncertainty for us, but not for God. For God, everything is settled, and so we look to God to give us the answer when we are sick or when our children are sick."

I think back to the fact that I didn't look to God during Abby's hospitalization. In fact, I barely looked to my parents while she was in the hospital. I looked almost exclusively to those I thought were the demigods who wore white coats around me, and by the end of our stay, even they didn't have the answers.

The rabbi tells me that the problem with the idealization of looking to a parent figure in this type of crisis is that it turns us into children. And this can only serve to keep us from moving forward because it is precisely the reverse direction of evolution, of growth. He tells me that, instead, we can look to the extraordinary people and events around us, to the angels walking among us. This is anything but rejecting religion, but rather seeking faith in our surroundings, in our everyday helpers, in our nurses and doctors, in our friends and family, in community, instead of relying on an unknown singular figure who may or may not be able to answer questions or provide miracles.

But if I am not looking to a singular comfort-giving framework in religion, is it still religion? Absolutely. It is faith, regardless of its source. It is finding it, as the rabbi tells me, in other parts of life where God may exist. That framework simply may not be a singular figure in a proverbial heaven for everyone.

Still, I am curious about religions outside of the Judeo-Christian helix.

An old colleague from Texas puts me in touch with an imam in Houston so that I can learn more about the Muslim perspective on the subject matter. Though many of his sentiments echo what I hear from Sophie and other Catholic and Muslim friends, it is powerful and resonant.

The imam tells me that if someone comes to the mosque looking for comfort, they can pray and comfort sick loved ones and remind them that "this is a trial from God." Everything, he tells me, is the will of God. He tells me that so many of the prophets, indeed, went through serious health issues. They were constantly supplicating to God about their health, and as a result, God responded to their prayers.

He tells me that there are verses in the Koran that teach you that if there is a fever, it is actually a cleansing of sin, and that there are others that indicate that if you die of certain illnesses, you are considered a martyr in the eyes of God. Fever, a cleansing of sin, the knowledge that something is wrong within the body, has long been a truth paramount to both religion and medicine, hearkening back to Hippocrates's proposed theories.

And yet, there is hope, he tells me.

"There are certain things we cannot know," he says. "But there is always hope, as well. That's what religion is. Hope to be a better person. Put our faith in the hands of God. Even if we lose everything, we have this hope that God will not waste our efforts. And it will always be paid back then in the life hereafter."

Hinduism is fueled by a belief in reincarnation, that an individual's soul is reborn in a new physical body time after time in an ongoing cycle of rebirth until that soul reaches a state of perfection and evolution. It does this through karma, which literally means "action" or "deed." Karma is a cause-and-effect paradigm, in which effects of good and bad deeds are returned to the soul in a future life. With an ongoing life, a renascent soul, these larger philosophical questions inevitably change. The uncertainty that a person faces perhaps may be less about what happens to the physical body, and as a result, less about the medical portion of it. After all, the physical body is what is treated in medicine.

The concept of reincarnation fascinates me. Its tenets return to a duality in nature. Hinduism retains a belief in many gods, yet still one supreme being. It is at once a monotheistic and polytheistic religion, with millions of deities that are individually interpreted versions of the supreme Brahman. Each deity is projected to serve an individual purpose. For example, the Indian goddess Durga, one of the most powerful deities in Hinduism, is a woman depicted in many books and films as a fierce warrior. She is drawn often with eight or more arms, and she battles evil and emerges triumphantly. Her tales are written widely, and it is said that upon hearing the stories of Durga, one is cleansed from sin. Perhaps one is cleansed from injury and illness, too.

I have seen the image of Durga over the years, and she has always intrigued me. Each arm—be it eight, six, or eighteen (also a mystical number to the Jewish faith)—carries with it another symbol. One of strength, femininity, power. Somewhere to turn when in need, in times of the unknown. Whether Hindu, Jewish, Christian, Muslim, agnostic, or atheist, or any other faith, we all need symbols like Durga, even symbols like the Bake Sale, which can help when an express faith in a specific God is overwhelming, ambiguous, nonexistent, or variable across cultures.

WHILE WAITING BETWEEN THOSE TWO MRIs, the three months in which hydrocephalus would worsen or would not, in which brain surgery would be the outcome or would not, part of me wants to have Sophie's faith. That unflinching, relentless knowledge that all will be well. I don't want to hear anyone tell me that, though. I don't want to hear people recite stories of their sick relatives who turned out fine because I don't know if it will apply to me. They can't know either. The illusion of certainty, though attractive, is merely that for me: artifice.

While Abby was sick in the hospital, I did not pray. I did not rely on faith. But neither did I relinquish it. I did not forcefully remove it from my own life. I simply accepted it if present, neither welcoming nor excluding it, by placing the little rabbinical card in Abby's crib or reluctantly participating in the Bake Sale or speaking to the rabbi. Perhaps that is a form of faith on its own. After all, Abby's fever broke the night of the Bake Sale, and we were discharged two days later. Family members with whom I spoke months later told me that when braiding the challah, they felt as though they were a part of something bigger than themselves.

Waiting

I am in the waiting room before Abby's second outpatient MRI. Because this is Los Angeles, I see a famous pop singer dressed in what I can only imagine is "pop singer conservative wear." A white suit, covering her skin from head to toe, an oversized hat in matching material, painfully high heels. The pop singer is alone in the corner trying to stay anonymous. I don't like many pop stars, but I've always liked this one. I listen to her music. I've bought her albums. I sit far away and try not to look. She wants to stay quiet. I think she's in for a brain bleed, too. Everyone's in for a brain bleed, I assume. Everyone's in for a scan of the head, as if there is no other need for an MRI. Other people in the waiting room ogle her, and I can tell she's trying kindly to retain her sense of self, her composure. So private an experience played out so publicly.

Abby is placed under anesthesia once again. This is the test that will determine whether she needs brain surgery. This is the image that will untie the neurosurgeon's hands. It is slightly less difficult to watch than the previous time. She fights the anesthesiologist a little more, and again does not need intubation. She comes out of it fine.

This time, though, I must wait days for the results. I can't even remember how many because the hours rush together, yet the time is both blaring and burning on my calendar. I want it to come and I want it never to come. I want an answer, but I don't want *that* answer.

When the date of the appointment arrives, I place Abby in her car seat and drive around in circles for forty-five minutes before heading toward the hospital. I am looking for a McDonald's because I need french fries. My body craves the salt. I finally find one and sit in my car for less than two minutes until they are all finished. I crumple the white and yellow paper bag and toss it in the corner of the passenger seat. I drive toward the hospital. I am early. Instead of waiting in that room again, I drive another twenty minutes to find a second McDonald's, where again I sit in my car and eat the second large helping of fries. I don't care that my body is swelling from sodium or trans fats or cellulite. The salt satiates me. I need it.

The fries taste so good, I consider getting a third helping. I don't want to drive back to the doctor's office. But my phone buzzes. Neurosurgery appointment, it says. *In fifteen minutes.*

I pull my hair back and feel a knot at the base of my hairline. I ignore it, tying a band around it. I drive back to the hospital, park my car, and meet up with Amir. An hour later, we are called back for our appointment. This doctor is the one who gave the more promising second opinion about Abby's surgical prognosis.

The neurosurgeon attending and fellow begin to explain the latest results. They seem short with us, as if they have other places to be, but nowhere more important than here at the same time. It seems a cognitively dissonant reception. If the surgeon shows little professional interest in a case, it will likely mean that is only because there is no surgery to be ordered. That is something we want. The look of banality in his eyes. The quick rounding of Abby, signing off on the note in a few minutes' time. *An uninterested surgeon is a welcome surgeon,* Amir and I say silently to each other: a remnant of the last few years while waiting for his neurosurgeon to explain away the roller coaster headache.

"Things have stabilized," the neurosurgeon says. "We won't need to place a shunt based on these images and how she's doing now."

He points to the images that are exactly like the ones from three months earlier.

"That's an indication that she'll continue to do well. I think you could be out in the clear in a year. Maybe two. We'll just watch it."

I hold Abby. I hold her tightly to my chest and I kiss her forehead and her ears and her hair and her eyes. I try to see myself in them. I never realized how almond my own eyes are until giving birth to Abby. Average in size, they come together on the outer edges like two swoops of a slide. The only difference is that hers are a crystalline blue, taken from my paternal grandmother, a survivor of Auschwitz, after whom she's partially named. "The eyes, the eyes," people say, when they look at the two of us together. It took me thirty-five years to realize how I really look.

The neurosurgeon tells us that Abby does not need surgery now, but that they'll repeat the MRI in another three months.

Another three months of waiting, flattened with each passing test. A fully blown balloon losing air with every season. Eventually, that balloon will lie flush, airless, no longer floating above our heads as a reminder.

This neurosurgeon is the ambulatory encyclopedia I imagined all doctors to be when I was ten years old. So is his protégée, the neurosurgery fellow we met in the hospital months earlier. They both speak to me and Amir with respect.

"People can live normal lives with literally half a brain," the fellow tells me. "We've done hemispherectomies before."

"Really?" I say, amazed at the science. "Is that what we are looking at, though?"

"No," she says, nodding. Not even a little bit.

If this is her attempt at calming us, I could give her a handful of other suggestions. And yet I'm divided. I know she's trying.

The salt from the french fries slips out of my underarms and speckles under my breasts.

"No surgery," I say calmly, taking it in. I'm still not overjoyed. This doesn't mean never. It means *not right now*. We'll need to redo all this again in three months.

"And we still don't know why this happened?" I ask.

"It was probably an AVM," they both say, "but we can't know for sure. Either it was and it burst, or it was something else."

I am starting to hear that phrase a lot from specialists we've visited over the weeks. Neurosurgeons. Neurologists. Hematologists. Ophthalmologists. Pediatricians.

An *arteriovenous malformation*. A fancy sibling of the aneurism, an AVM is a malformed collection of veins and arteries that can cluster and either lie dormant or burst, causing a potentially catastrophic bleed.

We nod.

"Yes, it's possible," they say.

"Probable, in fact," they say.

"But we can't know for sure," they say. "Let's look and see if we find any other AVMs in the scans," they say.

Amir and I listen and nod. We've been told that this is another reason we keep having MRIs every three months. Not only to monitor for hydrocephalus, but also to look around and see if they can find any AVMs sitting there like grenades, and if they do, then they can do something about it early on. Go in and clip it or embolize it before it bursts. So far they haven't found any (other) AVMs in there, but they keep searching. They discuss the small possibility of having Abby undergo an angiogram, a much more dangerous procedure on such a small child, but one that would offer a more complete picture of the brain. It is not recommended at this point. It is far too dangerous for her, particularly when there is nothing clearly indicating that there may be (other) AVMs. So the question will again be posed in another three months.

I walk out of the office with Amir, and we get back into the car as if nothing new is learned. We sit in the car silently, staring at the parking lot attendant a hundred feet before us. I smile. Amir's head drops to his headrest and he looks up. I place my hand out and Amir grabs it. We look back to Abby. She is near slumber. Contentment pours through us in the nothingness that is today, the banality of stability.

I don't cry. I play with the knot at the base of my hair. My necklace latch is stuck in it. It pulls at my scalp like the back of my head is fastened onto a meat hook. I don't bother to remove it.

Another three months of waiting.

HOURS LATER AT HOME, I google "hemispherectomy" and see a story on YouTube about it. The headline: **MEET THE GIRL WITH HALF A BRAIN.** Before reading the article or seeing the video, it already feels misleading, sensationalized. I watch a little girl of perhaps eight chat with poise and maturity as she sits in front of Ann Curry on the *Today* show's couch telling her extraordinary story. She is friendly and happy and beautiful and thriving. They run a story about her severe seizure disorder called Rasmussen's syndrome, and suggest that removing nearly half of her brain may have been the only option for a functional life. When she was experiencing up to ten violent seizures a day, her quality of life was poor. The removal of half of her brain was a preferable prognosis to this one, and so her parents agreed, relying on the ever-hopeful phenomenon of neuroplasticity at such a young age.

Doctors at Johns Hopkins surgically removed most of the right hemisphere of her brain when she was six, and she woke up paralyzed on the left side of her body. Within days, she was in physical therapy, and within months, she was walking and running and playing and speaking.

Her father is interviewed. "I truly believe that miracles happen, and my daughter is an example of that," he says.

Experts discuss the phenomenon of neuroplasticity, and the little girl speaks intelligently about it. She wants to be a ballerina. She will likely walk with a limp and not regain full control of her hand, but still she is walking and dancing and using her hands, and nobody is telling her that ballet is not possible now.

I continue googling. Another young boy had a hemispherectomy for similar reasons, and now he's playing sports and running around his regular school with his little brother living a normal life.

The key factor is their age, their youth.

I don't know if these stories provide me with comfort. I consider calling up the families to speak with them, but they don't want to hear from me. Our story is nothing. A two-week NICCU stay with no surgery thus far. A fever. To them, we are a scrape on the knee. To other families I meet in our everyday lives, we are the hemispherectomy.

I am starting to feel grateful for being nothing.

But we still have another MRI ahead. We still need to wait for Abby to hit her milestones, and the ones that come after that and the ones that come after that.

Amir says he could have figured out what happened to her if he had a full brain, if the cyst wasn't in there supplanting part of it. After all, his arachnoid brain cyst had only recently been discovered, despite forty years of latency.

He laughs. I only sort of laugh. I wait.

I feel the knot at the base of my hairline. By the time Abby goes through three MRIs and three additional neurosurgical visits with two different doctors and is well into her physical therapy, I cannot ignore the knot anymore. It's a full-grown dreadlock.

I joke with my friends, inserting it into conversation as if it's all part of the *new mom thing,* trying to feel normal, like one of them. "You know," I say, "the new mom thing where you don't have time to shower or whatever so you develop dreadlocks."

They look at me and laugh.

"That's not a thing."

I chop seven inches from my hair.

Control

A friend of mine from college is a public health researcher for a think tank whose work centers on, among many issues, public health emergency preparedness. She tells me that her world is reactive. In public health, it's about giving people a choice and then persuading them to act on it. For example, each year the new flu vaccine is released based on studies of the previous years of flu strains and the best possible guess for which strain will be prevalent that year. It's not possible to attack every strain of the

flu in the annual immunization, but the goal is to attack the largest and most populous strains expected. Still the flu vaccine is a
measure of real control. Though reactive, health professionals
are still actively taking control as much as possible given countless variables.

The reality is that public health professionals who make decisions for the mass population often have to act in the absence of
information. They sometimes must wait for something to occur
in order to fully prepare for the next crisis. Inaction is a type of
action, yet paradoxically, it is terrifying to live in a world where
you cannot necessarily prevent future catastrophes. You have to
wait for them to happen in order to prepare for the next.

Our bodies, our psyches, are also reactive. Once we get the
chicken pox, for example, we can work on not getting it again.
Our immunity builds. Once there is an injury, we cannot turn
back time. We can only prepare for the next one.

Guilt v. Blame

My father, a physician who consistently defends the physician's perspective, calls to give me his opinion that the initial
hospital we visited should not have allowed Abby to go home that
first time, when my brother and I brought her into the ER for
pyloric stenosis. Similarly, many of my attorney friends come
calling with their respective "Tell me when!" calls to action. I
even heard that one of the neurosurgeons we visited was also

surprised that the first ER let Abby go home at the time. I don't want to think about this. It's too soon. It doesn't matter. It doesn't change anything. But still the texts spill in.

Most physicians are sued at least once before they hit the age of forty. This is not necessarily due to actual malpractice, but rather to the inherent complexity of the work. Mistakes can sometimes be made without intent and even without the possibility of prevention. When something goes wrong, there is almost always guilt. And when lawsuits arise, blame becomes the guiding force to operate on that guilt.

When I was eighteen, my father was sued for medical malpractice for a case that proved blameless in nearly every capacity. Accordingly, not a single attorney took on the case, let alone ruled against my father, but nevertheless, because of that lawsuit, the hospital where my father worked took away his privileges to practice medicine. With a loss of identity, livelihood, decades of training, and limited funds, my father decided to sue the hospital to right his own wrong, displacing the blame in order to get his name, reputation, and livelihood back, and it was this lawsuit— not its source—that devastated our family financially and in many ways, personally. We lost our home and bank accounts—of course, incomparable losses to what other families lose in legitimate malpractice cases. Yet because of this, I learned at an early age that lawsuits are based not always on guilt, but on blame. When blame is not easy to spot, they are filed because of the need to learn the full story. After years, my father was eventually able to move past the lawsuit and continue practicing the medicine he loved so dearly. He found new hospitals in which to work, additional outlets beyond general surgery to help others, discovered a joy in working in small-town emergency rooms in need across Texas, and embraced a renewed sense of purpose despite the outward bruises.

Nevertheless, this conceit crystallized in early 2012 when I moved to Los Angeles and took a job as a medical malpractice defense attorney at a midsize law firm. That one year alone decimated thirty-three years of complete trust in the medical establishment as my everyday focus became the exception to the medical norm. The infinitesimal percentage of things going wrong became the one hundred percent focus of my daily life. I saw lawsuits flying in where no fault could possibly be found. I saw families drained and mourning as they longed for answers. I saw physicians devastated by split-second decisions that they believed were right at the time. I did also see malpractice, actual wrongdoing on the part of institutions and physicians where blame and guilt properly belonged, but this was far less common than the undeniable sadness of both parties wishing their time was spent anywhere but with us. I worked on cases that re-created fear of medicine, hospitals, and surgeries where my childhood mantra of "just an appendectomy, no big deal" was so deeply entrenched.

One case remains with me, years later. The defendant: a young man working as an anesthesiologist, happily married. His wife is pregnant with their first child, and a few weeks after giving birth, he returns to his work. He is scheduled to perform anesthesia on a case for an elective surgery. He goes into work as he has for years. Sure, he had been dizzy for weeks by the time of this particular surgery, but that is because he is a new parent. This change in temperament, this sleeplessness, all comes with the territory of new parenthood. Given his work, it is vital that he sleeps sufficiently, that he does not come to work exhausted. The slightest movement in the wrong direction could result in catastrophe.

There is another young man—kindhearted, eager to start his own business, a devoted husband and father. He elects to have surgery to combat his battles with obesity. Though it's usually a straightforward operation, this surgery still carries with it risks and complications, as do all surgeries. He signs waivers, is prepped, and looks forward to a better future professionally and personally.

The anesthesiologist begins to administer the anesthetic. Though a bit more exhausted and dizzy than usual, he is well trained to perform his job. He has performed this work hundreds of times and under far more stringent conditions than exhaustion.

This time, though, the anesthesiologist places a tube in the wrong anatomical airway, and as a result, the patient can't breathe. Numbers are flying in the wrong direction on the monitors, but not everyone catches the numerical anomaly in time. There is a lack of oxygen in the patient's brain for a period of time. The doctor doesn't quite catch the numbers slipping. He isn't communicating properly with his team, with the surgeon, with the nurses. The surgeon tries to help; he struggles to get oxygen to the patient, but it is too late. For that brief moment while the patient loses oxygen, he suffers anoxic brain injury. He is placed in a coma, and his future becomes unknown.

And yet the story, like all stories, is not that clear.

The doctor never comes home after the surgery. Following the mistake in the OR, the anesthesiologist realizes something must be very wrong, so instead of going home after the operation, he visits a doctor and discovers that it isn't new parent exhaustion causing his slip of the hand, but rather that he has been unknowingly suffering from a brain tumor. He spends the rest of his life in treatment centers, operating tables, doctors' offices, chemotherapy suites, and hospital beds.

The patient lives, and the family is able to focus on his recovery. In this time, he regains consciousness and with extensive rehabilitation, is able to learn how to walk and talk again, though never as well as before. While his condition does improve daily, he is disabled, requires home health workers, and loses a substantial amount of his future livelihood.

The anesthesiologist dies just over a year later, leaving behind his wife and new baby. The patient later sues the dead doctor's estate for malpractice.

Did the anesthesiologist make a mistake? Yes. But could he be ethically blamed? It is unlikely. There are no winners, no exculpatory individuals in this case, only people understandably looking for answers. Even in a potentially clear-cut case of malpractice like this one, where blame may be discernible, there still may be guiltless parties. How do we accept this reality when we need to make sense of an event catastrophic to so many lives?

Intellectually, I know things can go wrong in medicine, but even when they do, it is hard to accept that often nobody is at fault morally. Unlike criminal cases, medical malpractice cases present a window into an often blameless system of fault. And when that happens, what do we do with guilt? We turn it inward. Blame, though, somehow shifts the angle outward. It needs a scapegoat. It tells itself that it needs the law. In some cases, it absolutely does. But in most, the law is a poor substitute for closure.

I saw people—both patients and physicians—lose their livelihoods, their lives, their minds, all seeking one thing: exculpation in the narrative of litigation. Deeply, passionately, desperately seeking someone on a pedestal with a gavel, saying "guilty" to someone other than themselves.

I saw my father do it in my childhood for years as the arguments with my mother escalated and the numbers in their bank account dwindled. Until all of their children left home and tried to move past this "fourth child," this lawsuit that served as nothing more than a need to place certainty in a world where there is none.

It didn't take long in my practice of law to realize that the main reason people sue is not for money, but for answers. True, there is a hefty group of individuals who sue purely for money, perhaps motivated by revenge or greed or often the necessity to pay bills, but tainting all of it is the need for answers. For discovery of truth, discovery of life. The early process in litigation is literally called "discovery"; it is a means by which people can investigate the truth about their injuries and health crises and find someone to blame, find a culpable party that is hopefully anyone but themselves. Often they do not find a clear and objective answer, and with no answer there is no certainty. This reality is one of the only truths: that sometimes there is simply nothing and no one to blame.

A cruel revelation for an attorney.

A beautiful one for a writer.

A necessary one for a parent or patient.

I NEVER RESPOND TO MY friends about suing. I explain the reality to my family, completing the legal analysis in my head in between medical assumptions. In law, there is a fairly clear formula for determining liability in negligence cases. Duty. Breach of Duty. Causation. Damages: All four elements must be met. It's as simple as that, no matter how complicated attorneys make it out to be. Even if there was a negligent breach of duty somewhere along the line, there is no connecting causation here. Nothing to prove. Nobody to blame, and as time passes, perhaps no real damages either. No way to connect the dots conclusively or even beyond the preponderance of the evidence. Nobody at whom to point the finger saying, *It's your fault*. Not even to myself. I have no answers to find. No blame to misplace. Money will not "make Abby whole," the presumptive language for monetary awards in civil lawsuits. She's already whole as she is. As am I.

Graduation

After five MRIs and countless visits to specialists and Days at the Salon, we are again in the second-opinion neurosurgeon's office with the same Disney movie playing from three, six, and nine months earlier.

The last few results have been good. Stability. The proverbial prayer for an uninterested surgeon.

The neurosurgery fellow is the first to speak. I ask her about all the potential long-term effects of a bleed of this gravity. Now that hydro seems less likely and neurosurgery visits are waning, I'm starting to think more about the neurological component, the long-term effects that have no solution with a scalpel. Google and the Mayo Clinic and Cleveland Clinic and Medscape and Medline and the NIH all tell me online of possible outcomes following a Grade IV bleed. All of these statistics associated with this range of outcome have guided me in and out of sleepless nights, holding my child close to my heart. *But they aren't examining her; you are,* I want to say to the neurosurgeon, before she cuts me off.

"You would have seen by now if there were those kinds of neurological problems," she says, practically laughing at the normal baby smiling and cooing before her. Abby, potentially escaping all of their statistical dictates.

Treat the patient, not the paper, I often think when I reload pages on the Internet. A modern derivation of Hippocrates's words: "It is more important to know what sort of person has a disease than to know what sort of disease a person has."

"Abby looks just great," she says. "Continue what you're doing."

We've heard that before. She does look great. But I want to know what may happen in the future. Will *great* sink to *good* and then *average* and then *poor*?

"And . . . she still may need a shunt?" I ask.

They smile.

What about the future? I want to know.

They never say a thing. She looks great, they remind me. They aren't going to give me a prognosis just because I want one. But—

"Don't quote me on this," the neurosurgeon says to us kindly, "but you've graduated from neurosurgery."

I think he says something more about this. Perhaps something along the lines of not needing to return, of Abby being in great shape, of a great nonsurgical result. I hold Abby in my arms tightly as he speaks, and the apprehension turns to joy, which turns to complacency, which turns to normalcy in the span of a second. I am holding Abby exactly as I held her minutes earlier. Nothing in those moments has changed. She is the same person she was before he graduated her. There is no thick metallic door out of which he has come wearing green scrubs and latex gloves, telling me she survived. There is no test she just took out of which she emerged triumphantly. Just a simple office visit in which nothing in our lives changed.

Amir wants to hold her, so I pass her to him, but again we do not embrace with relief. We do not sigh. We do not cry. We do nothing but complete the conversation as if it is just another doctor's visit continuing life in the same exact pattern. Only now she does not need neurosurgery and will not need another MRI in three months. Merely a one-year follow-up. We have graduated, but not completely.

When each visit presents the same result, the final disclosure isn't earth shattering. It is just a continuation of the same. With each subsequent MRI showing unchanged ventricle size, we sort of expect to pass the test. It feels like relief and satisfaction of hunger. The removal of a splinter. The first step dipping my feet into a pool. I can tell the water is warm, but I'm not entirely certain how I'll feel when I dive in.

We are in the neurosurgeon's office for less than ten minutes. It's as simple a visit as a checkup for a cough. We never see him again.

I SHOULD BE MORE OVERWHELMED with her surgical graduation given all of this, but the cognitive dissonance of the surgeon's words still rests peacefully over my head as if I have lost my ability to emote. As if my heart and head have lost the tubing between them.

I have not lost their connection, though. This I know. It is now cautious. It is rebuilding with small moments, just like a baby learning how to walk. My head connects with my heart outside of the surgeon's office when I see her at home, taking those proverbial steps and embracing milestones.

The four plates of her skull are now closed, fused together properly as they should at this age. But still, I touch her closed fontanelle out of habit, testing, feeling for a potential bulge.

WITHOUT THE IMMINENT FEAR of surgery, without hydrocephalus, without semi-weekly head measurements or frequent visits to ENT to test her hearing or vision, we are welcomed into nothing more than parenthood.

I run that same Google search of "uncertainty is" again, and it reveals the following: (1) "uncertainty is the normal state"; (2) "uncertainty is the essence of romance"; (3) "uncertainty is the refuge of hope"; and (4) "uncertainty is killing me."

The positive and the negative are still there.

Possibility and finitude.

Romance and death.

Abby is almost one year old. One of the two neurosurgeons still suggests a one-year follow-up just to be absolutely sure.

She is talking but not yet walking.

I'll feel better when she walks.

Part Three

CHRONIC

UNCERTAINTY

. . .

Chronic

1. Referring to a health-related state, lasting a long time.

2. Referring to exposure, prolonged or long-term, sometimes meaning also low-intensity.

—*Stedman's Medical Dictionary*

Intervening Early

In the late eighteenth century, a young boy of twelve was found naked, alone, and filthy near the forests in a mountainous town in the south of France, Aveyron. He was running on all fours, scavenging food, fearless and unaffected by the weather or terrain. The most recent winter had been the coldest in memory, and the boy had apparently survived without any clothing. He did not express cold or pain. Unable to speak in French or any other language, the little boy demonstrated no means of communicating or hearing, and did not present an interest in interacting with other human beings. His body was a treasure map of scars, signaling most of a life lived in the wild. An instant phenomenon, this boy—soon dubbed "The Wild Boy of Aveyron"—was brought to a group of scientists and educators in Paris within the year to be studied.

It was the year 1800. France and the rest of the Western world were transitioning eagerly between the Enlightenment and the Romantic periods, steering their intellectual compass into investigations of human nature and medicine and psychology. Was this boy who resembled a human being in all physical capacities, who was clearly a child of the civilized though raised *without* civilization, still a *man*? Were we, in fact, made from the fires of nature, or were we products of nurturing, per the long-debated philosophies of Jean-Jacques Rousseau? The scientific community of Paris—and beyond—wanted to know.

A young Parisian physician fresh out of training, Jean Marc Gaspard Itard, perhaps looking for a place to make his mark in this intellectually burgeoning time, took it upon himself to teach the young "wild boy" and brought him home to live with him. He set two primary goals for his time with the boy, whom he named Victor: first, to teach him language, and second, to teach him empathy.

Itard began working with Victor on language and socialization. Notably, Itard wanted him to be able to use language to communicate even if written down or through hand signs. Initially, Victor was unwilling. He felt more comfortable mute and naked, where his body told a laborious narrative—where words failed—of how he came to be found in the woods. More puzzling than the haphazard scars and scrapes, though, was a large and very defined scar over his neck, indicating the possibility of intentional harm. This specific detail indicates that there was a possibility he was abandoned by his parents at the age of four or five. Perhaps those parents tried to kill him, deserting him so he could die in the woods following the gash in his throat, leaving him physiologically unable to speak. Or perhaps he was born with speech or behavioral problems, which might have prompted these parents to slash his throat and abandon him in the woods to die. After all, it was a time in which children who were unable to socialize within the norm were marginalized as "idiotic" or "imbecilic," and institutionalized or hidden from sight.

When Itard began to work with Victor, he was interested in removing a bit of that label. If children like Victor could be taught, he surmised, they could be civilized through a series of lessons. Itard observed Victor, determining his deficits and his needs, and created a detailed education plan specific to Victor, focusing on those specific needs through repetition of physical and verbal exercises and cues—essentially, behavior modification. Throughout this process, though, Victor frequently ran away back to the wild, where he felt more comfortable. Still, Itard persisted, constructing methods of repetition to create language. After nearly six years, Victor was able to verbalize two words: "lait," the French word for milk, and "Oh, Dieu!" (Oh, God!).

Sadly, Itard stopped working with Victor after those six years, believing he'd taken Victor's education as far as he could. Though Victor never learned to speak more than the two words, Itard's work enabled him to live a long life, even if not fully integrated into society. Following Itard's departure, Victor lived with a caretaker named Madame Guerin, who met Victor when she was Itard's housekeeper and likely aided him in the years of teaching. Victor moved in with her family and remained in their quiet care until his death in 1828 at the approximate age of forty.

Despite Itard's exit from Victor's life, Itard's contribution to psychology and education is profound. For six years, Itard documented every detail of the education, every procedure, every repetition, every development, and when he walked away, it was with the hypothesis that he simply got to Victor too late. It is this realization that was a critical moment in neuropsychology and education. Not only did he design learning strategies that were the historical precursors to our current systems of early childhood education, but he also opined that in order to teach viable language skills, we must intervene before adolescence. In other words, we must intervene *early*.

We cannot know with certainty if Victor was abandoned at the age of four or five *because* of his many behavioral or verbal issues, or whether they were the result of a life in isolation. The British novelist Jill Dawson fictionalized this story in her 2003 novel, *Wild Boy*, in which she contends that Victor was autistic, independent of the abandonment. American psychologist Harlan Lane argues in his comprehensive history of Victor and Itard, *Wild Boy of Aveyron*, that the work they accomplished together laid the foundation not only for special education, but for *all* education. Itard is now largely credited with laying the seeds of an educational movement emphasizing the significance of what we now call early intervention, in which a focus on examining a

child, determining that child's goals for development, and working early enough with that child through repetition can help
overcome many developmental delays. Of significance is the accepted ideology that these techniques also work as physical therapies for injured children in rehabilitation.

Over continents and centuries, this early form of education,
which began in Europe almost exclusively with the disabled, has
in turn become an adopted method for educating *all* children. Dr.
Maria Montessori, the founder of the omnipresent Montessori
schools over the globe, followed Itard's early teachings when
she created her own curriculum in the early twentieth century,
emphasizing the importance of individualized, child-centered
natural development. The school system is designed to create a
structured environment for children so that they can find their
own strengths and interests through, for example, uninterrupted
blocks of work time and guided choice of work activity. Teachers
are expected to observe each student and create individualized
plans that enable the children to develop their own strengths at
their own developmental pace and stage. At present, per the
North American Montessori Teacher's Association, there are ap-
proximately four thousand Montessori schools in the United
States and twenty thousand worldwide.

Regardless of intellectual level or socioeconomic status, in-
tervening early in development with children—with or without
disabilities, by finding their own way to work through play—was
recognized as real, an accepted therapeutic approach to helping
improve childhood development. So real that the United States

government codified the broad goals of early intervention into law in 1986 in the most sweeping legislation ever established for developmentally disabled children, providing "a statewide, comprehensive, coordinated, multidisciplinary, interagency." This bill, which has been amended over the years, provides services for children from birth to three years of age. Of note is the fact that though the federal government required funding for early intervention, it left the interpretation up to the states to determine what "developmental delay" means. In addition, it provided a discretionary category for "developmental risk." It is this final category of "at risk" children that includes injuries that may predispose a child to having developmental problems and therefore addresses them before they may emerge. It is this category that can become a catchall for children like Abby, who experienced a profound physical trauma in infancy.

I live in California, which is one of the states that provides funding for at-risk children. After an initial evaluation following Abby's discharge from the hospital, Amir and I throw ourselves into the world of physical and occupational therapy. After all, there is no other means of combatting any problems. There is no surgery, no medication that can suddenly undo a bleed. So a malleable program in which three different people visit our apartment four times a week is our best hope of either preventing or reducing any delays. Abby's program is structured around motor development.

Physical therapy focuses on gross motor skills, which, in infancy, include rolling over, crawling, walking, and, later, running, jumping, climbing, and riding a bike. Occupational therapy, on the other hand, concentrates on developing fine motor skills, such as twisting and pushing buttons, gripping, pulling, and turning, in addition to any sensory issues with, for example, sounds or touch. Toys, games. Swinging in swings and sliding down slides. Stacking blocks and drawing circles, horizontal lines, vertical lines. All activities she would do anyway in preschool or at home. Only now, someone is looking out to see that she is accomplishing those goals, that she is learning them properly. Someone is testing goals against a scale every six months, and so my uncertainty about her reaching milestones shrinks because I can see that she eventually meets them. I know weekly whether concern spreads across the faces of her kind therapists or whether excitement is the dominant emotion.

She begins at four months. The monitoring is extreme, four times a week, and when outside of it, there is nothing but everyday life, flecked with the confetti of parental neuroses and an overabundance of medical appointments. I see her develop. I see her mind expand. Amir, her babysitter, and I work with her daily, mimicking all of the exercises completed with her physical and occupational therapists. I learn what toys are good for fine motor skills, what invisible milestones she is meeting that otherwise would have just been life.

This is all we have. Tools as basic and as simple as our ability to communicate. Everything that Jean Marc Gaspard Itard had in 1800 France. No special devices costing millions of dollars to purchase. No lab coats and blood tests or surgical theaters. Just ourselves. And no way to prove any of it really works, or if it's just luck or happenstance. And so from her first few months, we all work with the therapists on play, on evening out any differences in muscle tone and strength from one side to the other, on smoothing out any sensory discomfort, on anything else that may arise in the process of these four-times-a-week house visits. Together we labor to ensure that despite this injury, through early intervention, she'll walk and talk and play like any other child.

Anniversaries

The *Oxford English Dictionary* places the etymology of the word "anniversary" to medieval times. The word, based in Latin and French, is traced across the centuries, meaning "returning with the revolution of the year; annual"; or "returning or commemorated at the same date in succeeding years."

"The word was at first ecclesiastical: 'Anniversary days . . . were of old those days, wherein the Martyrdoms or Deaths of Saints were celebrated yearly in the Church; or the days whereon, at every years end, Men were wont to pray for the Souls of their deceased Friends, according to the continued custom of Roman Catholicks.'" Over time, the reverent connotation has eroded, leaving only the commonplace acceptance of the word. *Return, annual, revolution, anniversary.* It indicates a cycle—not an end.

In Judaism, there is the concept of the *yartzeit*, which is the anniversary date of a loved one's death—usually for a parent, spouse, or child. On the *yartzeit*, the mourner lights a special candle for twenty-four hours to remember the dead. It is a constant reminder of what was lost and what was gained. The beloved's memory is always with us.

But what about the anniversary of a day that changed your life in other ways? How do we commemorate that?

On our seventh wedding anniversary, Amir and I learned I was pregnant.

"The seven-year itch," Amir's father said, with great affection.

English was not his first language. Amir and I looked at each other. "That's not exactly what it means, but yes, it's great news!"

I wasn't ready to have a child for many years and waited until my thirties until I wanted to even try. It took me more than a year to become pregnant, which in the grand scheme of things is not a terribly long time. During that year, Amir and I underwent fertility testing, which yielded no explanation as to what wasn't working. "Unexplained infertility" might have been written somewhere in a doctor's note. Nothing was discovered to be wrong with either of us, but it took longer than it should have to conceive. We began fertility treatments in an office with framed artwork of the enlarged anatomy of flowers. Two rounds of artificial insemination both met with failure. The week of the first insemination was the same week we learned of Amir's brain cyst. We questioned the plan. If he had a brain tumor, should we still try for the insemination? Did I want to still carry his child if he was going to face a short or uncertain future? Did I want to be a single mother? Could I care for both of them if necessary?

The decision was clear. We both wanted a part of him to live on, regardless of what the scans showed and regardless of the neurosurgeon's pending prognosis. I wanted him. I needed him. He wanted me. He needed me. We both wanted a child, equal parts us.

The morning he was wheeled into his MRI, which would eventually tell us that it was "just an arachnoid brain cyst," I walked to the women's health wing of the hospital to undergo a pelvic ultrasound to count my available eggs. Mine was clearly the less significant one, but both scans would give us a glimpse into our future, and both, we hoped, would display life. The answer was moments away, but in the space between, I was living outside my life and so very much within it. Waiting for test results does that to you. You are neither one nor the other, but a phantom version of yourself—living a partial life, neither embracing nor rejecting it. Just waiting for it.

Exhausted, unkempt, not knowing for those few hours what either of our scans would show, I told my OB everything. She hugged me, telling me that the valedictorian of her Johns Hopkins Medical School class also had an arachnoid brain cyst, which had been found incidentally on the free scans they got in medical school. "They're nothing to worry about," she said. "It will be fine. Do you still want to proceed today?"

"Yes," I said. "Let's see what's in there."

Less than three minutes later, I had an answer. My eggs were plentiful and ready for fertilization.

At the same time half a mile away, Amir was also getting an

answer. I wanted to run back to him and embrace. I wanted to tell him all will be well. I'm ready. Let's try this. You will be fine. You *are* fine.

When I walked to his room, he had already been wheeled back inside. His family was there, and I wondered if they knew where I'd been or thought I was an uncaring wife. The neurosurgeon told us more about Amir and was caring but unconcerned in the way you want your doctor to be caring and unconcerned. He didn't even request a follow-up. He merely looked at Amir as if he were a patient with a really bad migraine. I looked at Amir differently, and we both knew.

A week later, we completed our first round of IUI, also known as artificial insemination.

Amir was still recovering from the headache, and to a lesser extent from the appendectomy surgery. He joked again that if he'd had a full brain, he'd have invented Google. Or invented a way to circumvent the entire fertility process. He laughs about this frequently. I told him that his mind is working just fine. Except when it comes to musical theater. I think the part that enjoys musical theater and opera is sitting somewhere in the cyst, missing. See, I told him. I can joke, too. He kissed me and when he leaned over, I could see the pain caused from the slight movement.

Two weeks later, I bled.

We decided to take a month off from trying all the fertility treatments. Soon after, I became pregnant. "Spontaneous pregnancy," it's called. Spontaneity, according to nineteenth-century physicists, "is an enigma, a subject of profound astonishment." In the twenty-first-century world of infertility, pregnancy is called spontaneous merely because it's natural.

When we learned that I was pregnant on our seventh anniversary, it seemed an extraordinary sign, and we happily accepted the message.

But with the other anniversary coming up on the calendar, Amir tells me he doesn't want to think about it.

"Let's not make this a thing," he says. "It happened. She's doing well now. Let's not *commemorate* what happened."

And he's right on so many levels. But that's a moment that cannot be forgotten. How do we commemorate the past without mummifying it? Does a *yartzeit* candle commemorate the person's death or the person's life? The latter, certainly, but the act of lighting that candle requires acknowledgment and acceptance of the passing, creating a commemoration and not a mummification.

On the one-year anniversary of March 12, I remember because I want to remember how it felt when a date taught me that whatever happens next is manageable. Over time, March 12 will likely lose its poignancy in my life, and by the time this book is published, it may not even cause me to flinch. December 7 was once as powerful a date to most Americans as 9/11 now is. Even still, it pains me to know that so many younger friends do not look to 9/11 with the same sense of horror that I do, with the same panic I felt when I feared that my sister and my friends might have been lost. With time, those anniversaries, too, fade into the footnotes of life. So now when I look ten, twenty, fifty years into the future, a footnote is all I hope this will become.

Blood

There is an experimental form of visual art called Bioart, in which artists have merged their work with biology, by using (sometimes) live tissue, bacteria, other living organisms, and life processes to create works of art. It is at times a macabre art form that blends the experience of viewing and interpreting exhibits between art and science, cultural and sociopolitical criticism. The work is at once beautiful and horrifying, fascinating and controversial, necessary and toxic—just like blood itself.

Laura Splan is a New York City–based visual artist whose work explores the intersections of art, science, technology, and craft. Laura and I met while both in residence at an artist colony in Woodstock, New York, in the summer of 2010—she, working in visual art, and I, writing a novel. I remember strolling through her studio at the end of the month, drawn to her examination of the human body in its relation to expression. She was working on a project in which she was painting detailed designs of doilies that looked like old wallpaper, but with blood. Her *own* blood. These traditional patterns often found in homes function as a camouflage for the uneasy biological matter, evoking, as she describes, "a narrative of uncomfortable truths seeping through pleasing facades."

She tells me years later that she was interested in exploring the connections between domesticity and biological imagery. "Our relationship to both is so ambivalent," she says. "We have a sense of wonder at science and beauty at biological imagery, and the next moment repulsion of fear and discomfort."

But why the blood? Why your own blood? I want to know. Splan studied biology in college before becoming an artist, the result of an early interest piqued by a childhood peripheral to medical devices, since her father worked for a company that manufactured implants and surgical products. As an adult, she even became a certified phlebotomist so that she could draw her own blood for her work.

"I do that out of convenience," she tells me, "but also with a clear decision to redirect the conversation because I'm much more interested in exploring our understanding of the material of the body." Featuring blood as the artistic material inherently elicits all sorts of questions. "'Is it infectious? Whose blood is it?' It brings up our own fears about our bodies and the bodies of our fellow humans."

The art is detailed and beautiful, comforting and familiar, yet it also looks like microscopic biological agents, cells, diseases, an enhanced view under a microscope magnified on the wall, making us all microscopic organisms living within *its* world. Without reading the gallery card or description of the wallpaper or doilies, you wouldn't even know that it is made of blood.

"There always is a certain holding back in my work," Splan says. "To not let the viewer know the full story of an image. You would see a drawing with blood on paper, but not unless you read the gallery handout know that it is blood . . . [which is] part of the way uncertainty plays out in my work."

She hopes that the work triggers a question and hopefully more questions, and the uncertainty in that is infinite.

"It requires you to make a decision about how you feel," she says. "This alternates ambivalence and uncertainty. Maybe it's a cascade."

An unending, unanswering of questions. One leading to another and another.

"I've really tried to get at the sense of fragility," she says. "The precarity of the system . . . one little thing goes wrong and one little vein is out of place and it completely breaks down and fails."

I think back to all the times Amir talks about gout crystals under microscopes.

"They are gorgeous," he frequently says, sometimes wanting to enlarge the microscopic images as art on the walls in his office. This is no less or more macabre than Laura painting with her own blood. Maybe that is the ambivalence. The bifurcated nature of the substance. Of the body. Of life.

The details of brain scans, too, are so intricate, so full of waves and dots. As are Laura's designs. Each tells a story. Each beautiful and terrifying, destructive and necessary, comforting, familiar.

White is no longer the predominantly obtrusive object in Abby's scans. Any blood that was there has since reabsorbed into the brain. We settle on a word for what happened: "stroke." It is the most commonplace explanation. The one I can wrap my head around. The one people have every day. The one that debilitates some and does nothing to others.

The fact that blood can be so vital to our body is clear. It is made up of four components: plasma, red blood cells, white blood cells, and platelets. The fact that when in the wrong place, blood can be so dangerous is something that baffles me. The fact that it doesn't always permanently destroy the body when displaced is even more perplexing. When blood flows through vessels, sixty thousand miles of avenues within the human body, it is substance, fuel, a four-part fluid essential to life; but when it slips out of its proper channel and spills, it can become toxic. A bruise is merely an underground bleeding of the body that never made it to the surface. It follows a colorful course. Black. Blue. Brown. Yellow. And then back to normal. Life at its most precarious, its most fragile state.

San Francisco

Interstate 5 unravels before me for six continuous hours. From Los Angeles to San Francisco, I drive through the day without more than a few hours' plans. Spontaneity has been my preferred style for years, but with a child, it becomes less and less viable.

The Aneurysm and AVM Foundation (TAAF) is a nonprofit organization, "dedicated to bettering the lives, support networks, and medical care of those affected by aneurysm and other vascular malformations of the brain," according to its Web site. It is a volunteer organization run by survivors, caregivers, and medical professionals, and is hosting its Tenth Anniversary Walk beneath the Golden Gate Bridge in San Francisco in forty-eight hours. I've been wavering for days about driving up to participate in it. The Aneurysm and AVM Foundation is all about brain hemorrhages, aneurysms, burst or otherwise, arteriovenous malformations, burst or otherwise, and every rare collection of vascular brain abnormalities in between. This walk will be a communion of hundreds of people from around the country who have experienced the trauma of a bleed or the uncertainty of wondering if they would suffer a bleed at any moment's time. Up until this point, I have not spoken with anyone else who has gone through a similar medical trauma and come out on the other end alive.

I learn about it from a friend of a friend who has been living with a wrongly diagnosed terminal brain tumor that was actually a cavernous brain malformation (which is sort of like a dripping aneurysm). Hers is resting in her brain stem, a particularly dangerous location. She doesn't know if or when it will burst. She has refused surgery to clip it at this point because it is in such a vital part of her brain and she does not want to risk possible damage from surgery, and so she tries homeopathic remedies to help with symptom loss and continues on with her daily life. She's a fully functional, intelligent, charismatic, social young woman who works for the government. Initially, she had headaches and a seizure that led her to believe something was wrong, but after months of misdiagnosis (from multiple sclerosis to the brain tumor), she ultimately learned her reality. She doesn't know what her future holds, but she is continuing on with her daily life until she cannot.

When she tells me about the walk, I question my own motives, my proper place. After all, we may not really fit into this community. We don't know what caused Abby's injury. All we have is "AVM" as the leading contender on every doctor's differential that can be neither proved nor disproved. If it was one, it burst, and we can't prove a negative. If it wasn't, then we still don't know what caused the bleed. Each time we visit the imaging center for another MRI, the new anesthesiologist reviews her chart and arrives at the same summary.

"So she hasn't had any additional seizures since the incident?"

"No."

"And they didn't find a source?"

"No."

This is why Abby continues to have MRIs beyond the resolution of the hydrocephalus—to see if they can find any others, to make sure that the growing brain hasn't hidden any small AVMs, despite our graduation from two neurosurgeons. They haven't found any.

Still, we hear, "It looks like it was probably an AVM" every time before anesthesia.

When I hear the word "probably" in this context, I think of Sanford, an old high school acquaintance who was plagued by hypochondria. Sanford spent much of his senior year at home, poisoned by his own mind. Both agoraphobia and hypochondria took over his life. It wasn't until years later, with time showing him that he does not in fact have any of the diseases he believed, that he was able to move past the hypochondria, or at least past the acute uncertainty that plagued him during those years, while the passage of time and therapy aided in his agoraphobia. He eventually became a "hoop troop" entertainer for a professional basketball team, tossing out T-shirts, revving up the rowdy crowd for the basketball team. In front of twenty thousand people a night on a Jumbotron and on broadcast TV, Sanford embraced a personal challenge to overcome his agoraphobia by accepting a very public challenge. He wanted to take control of his life. But still, he told me, "the single word 'probably' is just enough uncertainty to act as a gateway to a daily struggle within my own mind and body."

Though this is anything but an imagined injury, the concept is the same. "Probably" leaves questions unanswered, carving out a cavity of anxiety for him. And for me, too.

"Yes," Amir and I nod, agreeing with almost every medical professional, when they land on this diagnosis. "Probably an AVM."

The diagnosis, or lack thereof, is just some sort of language with which to grasp some sort of reality. I even start to use this acronym in my daily conversation as if everyone knows what it means.

But when this friend tells me about The Aneurysm and AVM Foundation walk, I want to support her, so I donate to her team's fundraising page. I don't think of going until late on the Friday afternoon before the walk when I call the organizer of the event to learn more.

"You should come for yourself!" she cheers. "You'll be so glad you did."

I then told her what had happened to Abby. I've gotten used to explaining this in one line.

"I *should* come," I say back to her, convincing myself in the process.

"Call me if you need anything," she says. Her name is Susan.

Several hours later, just prior to midnight, I book a hotel and the next morning drive 383 miles with Abby in the car seat in the back of my car.

I made this drive earlier in the year for public readings for my novel. But in just a few short months, the vast devastation to the state from its water crisis is evident. Broadcast over the news for the country to scrutinize, to pity, to blame for overuse of our precious water supply, evidence of the severe drought surrounds me in yellows and crisp oranges, a burned landscape aching for sustenance.

Early into the drive, mixed in with the dying landscape, is a canvas of palatial scope, housing thousands of cows. It isn't possible to see how far back this cow farm stretches, but there are so many grazing animals, they spot the side of the highway like freckles. Still, it is the smell I remember most from my earlier drive, a putrid sort of fertilizer that climbs into my car and travels with me all the way north.

Mixed between the cows and the perfectly curated vineyards are small trees collected in straight lines and short mountains. Arid hills that didn't seem to make the final transition into mountainhood. I cut through them on my way. They sit to my left, while the fresh bushels of grapes grace my right. The beginning and end of life, I think, with movement sandwiched between. I drive forward and dozens of miles later, the desert hills are dry and arid. No unruly trees, no vines growing on them. Land just sitting there crunched together like Rodin's fist. The earth's knuckles, contemplating, thinking.

ABBY AND I WAKE UP early the following morning after a night in a hotel and drive to the Golden Gate Bridge. I park my car and wander around the parking lot, stumbling into two other organized races in the same area that morning. Just beyond a marsh and closer to the majestic bridge is Crissy Field, a midsize plane of grass with twenty or so white tents and a table for registration. Signs with ANEURYSM AND AVM FOUNDATION are posted everywhere I can see. This is where we are supposed to be.

I whisper to Abby.

Let's go.

I push her stroller onto the grass and walk forward. My adrenaline spikes as though my body knows what to expect. It recognizes this scene. In the past six years, I've slipped into running shoes for nearly a dozen amateur races, half-marathons, 10Ks. The early morning registration, the tents full of bananas and bagel strips, Gatorade and water spilling out of small paper cups. The potpourri of movement, activity, progression. As I walk closer to the tents, my chest begins to tighten. The size of the tents grows and my eyes narrow. Tears I don't even know still reside within me are suddenly awakened, beginning to form somewhere deep in my chest, in my throat, finding their way onto my cheeks without my even realizing it.

I haven't cried—at least about Abby—in almost a year. The emotional pathways have not been blocked, at least not consciously. They've been played out in my writing, in speaking with doctors, Amir, my friends, and family. In speaking with others who had experienced traumatic medical uncertainty or traumatic medical crises in a loved one following hours of conversation. In discussions of rational and logical pathways to coping. In reading, in writing, in living. None I've met—up until now—has survived a brain hemorrhage. A Grade IV hemorrhage, no less.

I approach the registration tent and wipe away my tears.

"Survivor or caregiver?" a woman says to me, as we wait in line to fill out paperwork.

I stare at her as if she isn't speaking to me.

She asks again.

"Survivor or caregiver?" she says, pausing, as if mortified by her own question. "Or . . . in memory of?"

A magnetic woman in what appears to be her forties, she is wearing a Wonder Woman shirt and cape. She looks like she is in charge. I wonder if she is Susan.

"Survivor . . . ?" I say, split, but motioning to Abby, who is observing the scene, soaking in the people, the early morning bay breeze.

"I don't really know what we are. I mean, we don't exactly fit.

She had a brain bleed at six weeks and"—I say, stalling, starting to tear again; tears that I didn't access for so long rise in my body and spill again to my face; I try to finish—"though we don't know what caused it." I continue: "The leading contender is that it was an AVM."

"Oh, sweetie," Wonder Woman says to me, hugging me. She is tearing up, too.

"This is her?" she asks, pointing to Abby.

"Uh-huh."

"How old?"

"Six weeks," I say again, breaking into more tears. "I mean she's fourteen months now, but . . ."

She embraces me another time, and we hold each other for longer than two strangers should. I don't want to stop. I think I'm supposed to stop, but I can't. My arms need to wrap around her.

"She's a survivor. She gets a survivor patch. Here!"

She hands me a cloth patch with the word SURVIVOR stitched into it, along with the Aneurysm and AVM Foundation logo and Web site. Together we remove the back of it and place it on Abby's shirt.

"I had a burst aneurysm about five years ago," she tells me. "I was in the Adirondacks with my family and it hit me like a truck in the back of my head. Thank God my kids weren't around. I don't remember anything after that. I spent three weeks in the hospital having my brain drained."

She laughs through the whole story. Through the tears, the smiles, the cool breeze.

"I don't remember any of it," she says again. "Thank goodness I don't remember."

I can't help myself. I embrace her again.

"I'm so, so sorry," I tell her. "You are incredible. Wonder Woman indeed."

"Right?" she says, laughing. "I thought the cape worked."

"It does!"

She looks again at Abby, smiling.

"And now . . . ?" I ask.

"Now I am doing well. I struggle with numbers, but I'm grateful to be here."

Wonder Woman, I soon learn, flew into San Francisco from the Midwest with her best friend to do the walk and to celebrate their birthdays together. This is the second year in a row that she's done the walk. She tells me that people have flown in from all over the country for it as it is the only one of its kind for AVMs, bleeds, and other vascular malformations.

I tell her that I just found out about it and that I decided on Friday night that I would come. I drove up on Saturday morning and would drive back to Los Angeles later that day, Sunday, after the walk.

"With . . . a baby?" she says, close to shock.

"Well, she's sort of toddler-y now," I say, laughing. She has just begun to walk, and though nearly fifteen months into her small life and the fact that she's experienced more than most adults, at least medically speaking, she's still caught somewhere between toddlerhood and babyhood.

"By yourself?" Wonder Woman asks. "You drove six hours alone with a baby two days in a row straight . . . for this?"

"Yes," I nod.

She hands me another survivor's patch.

"Here," she says. "You deserve one of these, too."

I WALK AROUND the partitioned areas, eating bananas and feeding them to Abby, while taking in the scene. It isn't large. Fifteen tents, maybe fewer, maybe more, square a small area of Crissy Field. There are tents with memorials flanking their entrance, large photos of loved ones lost due to a stroke or some other form of brain hemorrhage. The unlucky ones. Caregivers, nurses, doctors, and survivors congregate together below the Golden Gate Bridge. I hear their words as a Greek chorus.

I still have trouble with words, all these years later. I am losing language.

I still have trouble with numbers.

Sometimes I forget things more than I did before.

I am lucky that I have no deficits, but I still struggle with PTSD.

Though these troubles, major or minor, follow many like shadows, there is a sense of camaraderie—community and love and support. Everyone wants to speak and share. This is not a group of people who came through with such debilitating damage that they are unable to travel and share their stories publicly, and so it is undoubtedly a self-selecting group. They are most likely the ones who came through on the other end visibly unscathed, partially unscathed, or with limited to no long-term effects. Invisible trauma. Trauma in another form.

These survivors, the ones who may have memory or language or numerical loss, often have no substantial visible cognitive or motor loss. For the most part, this is the group of people who are able to walk five kilometers, even if slowly. This is the group whose parents and friends cling to each other in gratitude. This is the group whose community reminds us that it is important to connect, to speak. Those with profound brain damage resulting from a burst AVM or aneurysm may or may not be here. I don't know. Many people who are here are like Abby and me. And for the first time in more than a year, I don't feel alone. I am at peace, regardless of what transpires next.

When the walk ends, everyone gathers on the field to listen to survivor stories. Hearing many of the stories spoken aloud gives me and everyone there, I assume, a sense of validation and connection. And yet, part of me feels like a voyeur as a parent whose child is diagnosis-less. Perhaps I've always felt like a voyeur. When we return to neurosurgery appointments or visit the old NICCU to say hi and show how well Abby is doing, I feel as though we don't fit in. At fifteen months, after a year of physical and occupational therapy, she is already speaking, recognizing her colors, and counting to ten. She is frequently tested against other normatives in her weekly therapies, and halfway through her first year of rehabilitation, we learn that her verbal and cognitive skills exceed her age, even if her motor skills are slightly lagging. I'm not worried that she won't eventually catch up. The state of California already wants to cut her hours of physical therapy in half because they claim she no longer needs them.

I hug the other parents on the course. Though I am the same age as many of the participants, I am not a survivor. I am a parent. A member of an entirely different tribe.

Survivors

On my drive home from San Francisco, Abby sleeps, and I am able to think clearly. I pass the knuckled mountains and cow farms. I pass the lush greenery in Northern California before stretching back through the drought-laden Central and Southern California inroads. It is later than the previous day's drive. A full moon, yellow in its starkness, sits low in the light-blue sky, instructing my direction home. I glance back at Abby periodically in the rearview mirror. She is still wearing her SURVIVOR badge.

I hadn't thought of attaching that word to her before. It is powerful yet divisive, and so drenched in pride. Survivorship implies completion, a termination of one story and the beginning of another. It necessitates an ending. Does she, like all of these others, have an end to her story? Perhaps it is just a new story now rewritten, with this additional element included.

There is a powerful proprietorship to the word "survivor." Suffering, strength, will, tenacity, drive, belief, luck. Luck that this happened in the part of her brain that is redundant in size. Luck that it happened when she was six weeks old. Luck that it wasn't terribly large within the tissue, despite its mammoth-sized leak when combined with the intraventricular bleed. But despite luck and serendipity, could a one-year-old earn the right to be called a survivor? Is a premature baby a survivor? Aren't all babies, by that respect, survivors of the birth canal? What a profoundly primal experience it is to be born. Was it strength, will, and belief that pushed her to a position of health, or was it luck? Was it good doctors, early intervention, genetic predisposition, a support system?

Before driving home, I text Amir a picture of a smiling Abby in pigtails wearing the SURVIVOR patch. On the drive, we speak about it as the green mountains turn brown and darken into graphite.

"I didn't like it," he says to me. "I didn't like seeing that word on her."

I didn't verbalize it at the event, but I felt the same way.

"It doesn't feel right," I say.

Yes, technically she has lived past the bleed. She did not die, and in that she has survived, but the word doesn't seem appropriate, earned.

"I think of two things when I think of survivors," I say to Amir. "Holocaust survivors and—"

"Cancer survivors," he says, completing my thoughts.

"Exactly, and the problem with using that language with cancer is that they aren't necessarily survivors of cancer, but rather that they are in remission. The cancer is gone, but it may come back."

THE TINCTURE OF TIME

Susan Sontag discusses this reliance on the "military meta-phor" as applied to cancer in her landmark book *Illness as Meta-phor*. "However 'radical' the surgical intervention, however many 'scans' are taken of the body landscape," she writes, "most remissions are temporary; the prospects are that 'tumor invasion' will continue, or that rogue cells will eventually regroup and mount a new assault on the organism."

This is not to say that once someone is in remission, he or she has not survived that first bout—rather, that it is not actually over indefinitely. Once there is a finite conclusion, the language shifts into a greater military paradigm in which there is a victor and victim, winner and loser, survivor and prisoner of war.

Sontag writes critically of the military metaphor as ascribed to illness, specifically cancer. "There is the 'fight' or 'crusade' against cancer; cancer is the 'killer' disease; people who have cancer are 'cancer victims.'" The problem with this mode of thinking, she argues, is that despite the fact that the illness is the perpetrator, "the cancer patient . . . is made culpable." When you treat the disease as "a demonic enemy," she says, you "make cancer not just a lethal disease but a shameful one." If you win that battle with cancer, you are a survivor or a winner, but if you lose it, then by linguistic imperatives, you are a victim or a loser. Of course, you didn't do anything wrong. It's not that you didn't try hard enough. This is also not to say that there is no pride in completing chemotherapy or coming out of the other end of surgery or treatment cancer free. And certainly, it's not to say that we

shouldn't feel hopeful and optimistic during surgeries and therapies because we absolutely must. But we have ascribed such militant language to cancer and illness in general that the only other
option is the implication of weakness.

By establishing polarizing identities, militant imagery with
cancer and other illnesses and injuries identifies a common enemy,
but in the process suggests that if you have not defeated that enemy
in the battle, then you lost, you are weak, you aren't good enough.
The truth is the disease takes a hold of you, and there is sometimes
nothing you can do about it. You are a part of humanity, which
inevitably carries with it elusiveness, mystery, the unknown, no
matter how much society and medicine advance.

MY FATHER IS AN INFANT Holocaust survivor. Born in the Radom, Poland, ghetto in December 1942, he was hidden briefly by
his uncle's girlfriend, and then adopted and raised in rural Poland by another family for three years until the war ended and
my grandfather was able to track him down and win him back.
This story traverses many narratives: channeling business deals
on the Polish black market, an intense legal custody battle culmi-
nating with a win for my grandfather, blackmail, and the swift
flight out of the country so that the newly reunited family would
remain intact. My grandfather was on Schindler's List, though
he refused to participate in the original Thomas Keneally book
and subsequent Steven Spielberg film adaptation. My grandmother was an Auschwitz survivor and also a privileged member

of the "White Buses Initiative," a humanitarian mission and exchange with the German government. At the end of the war,
count Folke Bernadotte, a Swedish nobleman and diplomat saved
thousands of women, including my grandmother, in white buses
with large red crosses, taking them out of the concentration
camps to safety in the only neutral Scandinavian country in
Europe near the end of the war in 1945. Both of my paternal
grandparents survived the Holocaust on their wit, their physical
strength, the luck of their age, their location, their commingling
with Schindler and Bernadotte, their ingenuity, and the motiva-
tion to survive with the primary goal to find their son when it
was all over. This is the mythology of my life, the story I was
born to discover and at some point write, and it has informed so
much of my identity. I am the child of and grandchild of Holocaust survivors. After one day of knowing me, that fact will likely
slip into any conversation.

My grandparents were defined by their survivorship. Every
time I saw them, it would come up in conversation, and rightly so.
Though he was never in the camps, my father also survived the
Holocaust, was reunited with his parents at the age of three, moved
to Germany to await sponsorship to America, moved to Baltimore
at the age of seven, moved to Los Angeles at the age of eighteen,
became a doctor, was drafted into the U.S. Army, and served as a
MASH surgeon in Vietnam. He got married, had three children,
suffered triumphs and tragedies, and picked up new identities like
"grandfather" in the process. Yet through this extraordinary life,
he has not always considered himself a Holocaust survivor, but

rather the child of survivors. It is an important distinction. He remembers nothing, one could argue, so should it even apply to him? If we don't remember what we have survived, does it no longer count? By that logic, is Abby ever going to be a survivor?

Though emotional residue will forever attach itself to Holocaust survivors, there was an end to the war in 1945. A completion of a battle, a rescuing from an objective enemy imparting injury, illness, and likely death. If you were not killed in a concentration camp, then you survived. If you did not die of starvation, malnourishment, freezing, then you survived. The problem in ascribing these words we choose to medical conditions is that they can become flagrant and diluted when they don't fit perfectly. Survivorship requires a sense of certainty that medicine simply cannot offer, which is not necessarily a bad thing if it helps you cope. It must simply be kept at bay so that it is used as a coping mechanism and not false hope.

IT IS NOT FOR ME to determine that the word "survivor" should be used only in terms of battles or wars and not with respect to injury and illness. If it helps people, they should wear the label proudly. It simply did not feel accurate for us. When Abby is old enough, she can decide for herself if she even feels a connection to this time to determine if she identifies as a survivor. It may be an insignificant flicker of her past. This book and her folders of medical records far thicker than this book may be all she has to know of her own infant medical history. Like my father's connection to his birth in the Radom Jewish ghetto during a typhoid epidemic, instead it may feel distant, separate, something that is part of her mythology alone.

Amir and I speak about this for a majority of the six-hour drive, and when I pull into our garage, he meets me by my car and carries a sleeping Abby upstairs to our apartment. Together we peel off the sticker from her shirt. We bathe her, dress her for bed, kiss her, and tuck her into her crib, and she sleeps through the night.

The patch now sits in the same drawer with the rest of her hospital bands, her Get Well Soon cards, her MRI results and ultrasound photos. A constellation of identity, great and small, significant and insignificant. Details to be accessed when needed, or not needed. Perhaps never needed. This, the documentation of a life.

Resolution

Acute injuries and illnesses always resolve themselves, one way or another. They evolve into long-term maintenance or reframed normatives. Acute uncertainty does, too. As does the subacute period of waiting. Answers eventually reveal themselves through resolution, and you adjust your expectations. Or if they never do, then the unknown is the only known variable and you plan accordingly.

An old lawyer friend of mine, Adam, learned several years

ago that he is a genetic carrier for the rare degenerative neurological disease frontotemporal dementia (FTD), the same disease that killed his father in his early sixties, and likely his two uncles, his aunt, his grandmother, and maybe even his great-grandfather, though the latter cannot be proved. In this specific kind of FTD, a chemical begins to erode vital portions of the frontal and temporal lobes, affecting personality traits like empathy, usually in the carrier's early forties.

Sadly, FTD is often misdiagnosed as depression, anxiety, or anti-personality disorder because the personality is attacked before the body. Erratic behavior mixed with a gradual shift in outlook can be confused with a psychological or psychiatric disorder. Adam's father, a reputable architect, lost his job in his forties, and after a decade or so of fleeting jobs, an apathetic outlook on life, he was finally diagnosed with this disorder via genetic testing. At the same time his father was gaining clarity on his life, however, Adam was getting married and also gaining his own form of clarity. It seemed as though much of his life suddenly had an explanation with respect to family dynamics and relationships. He was given new information that explained the past, and perhaps could even forecast a future.

Adam's biological family decided to participate in a large university study, tracking this disease over time. Each member was given the nearly impossible decision of deciding if he or she wanted to find out whether or not he or she was a carrier. Not all of Adam's family members wanted to know the future. They participated without requesting results of the genetic testing so that the university could follow them and track results, even while they waited. Instead of knowledge, they preferred to allow life to continue without the tarot card of the caduceus thus dictating it. Adam, though, wanted to know. He was getting married. He wanted to have children. He needed to make decisions based upon the science flooding his body.

With his fiancée by his side, he was given the results informing him that he is a carrier for this rare disorder. He told me that according to the genetic testing, there is a 100 percent chance he will get frontotemporal dementia, and he has a fairly clear timeline as to when symptoms will start to appear. He looks to his father as an example. After a decade or so of this erratic behavior, it was clear that Adam's father's frontal and temporal lobes had begun to decompose. The decomposition slowly crawled its way through the parts of the brain controlling emotions and eventually vital bodily functions such as the ability to swallow and eventually breathe. His father died at the age of sixty-two. Adam told me that he, too, expects to die in his early sixties.

Adam is a kind, generous, intelligent, and empathetic man in his midthirties. He is a husband and a father to two young boys, an attorney, a writer, an entrepreneur. When given the opportunity to learn more about his future, to eliminate some of the uncertainty surrounding his health, he chose knowledge and planning, eliminating that uncertainty because he could. In many ways, on the day he was given his diagnosis, he was given a sort of distorted certainty, the way mythological prophets can see into their own futures. He needed to know the future to write his own narrative. He was ready to serve as his very own oracle. The more information for him, the better.

Within years of this test, Adam changed his career trajectory. An attorney by trade and former college gymnast by passion, he gave up his legal job to open up a gymnastics school to teach children. He invested in a life insurance policy for his family. He downsized his housing costs. He made arrangements for his gym to be sold when he reaches a certain point of mental deterioration at which he knows he can no longer operate the business properly. He spends his days with his two young boys and his evenings teaching in the gym he built and renovated with his own two hands. He expects to begin to see degenerative effects in his forties and in the last years of his life to require caretaking by his wife, a teacher.

Together they have rewritten their narrative with the information provided to them at this point in time. Could it all change? Could there be a cure? Sure. In which case, he'll rejoice. There are still unknowns, of course; he doesn't know exactly when symptoms will start or if the foreknowledge that a disease outside of his control causing symptoms may help him combat some of his projected erratic behavior. For the most part, though, he is able to control so much more than he otherwise may have. He is now able to check off the list of things he's always wanted to do, knowing his clock is ticking loudly, but not so loudly that he can't accomplish a great deal in his twenty to thirty years left. Or his ten good years.

No doubt this dictate of a future touches his wife differently. For her, I think the uncertainty is jarring. She told me that she doesn't think about it all the time. But every once in a while, the reality of the diagnostic future creeps up on her. It is not something she frequently contemplates. She can't. Thinking about it all the time, worrying about it, well—

"That sort of uncertainty," she said to me, "is unsustainable."

Shrinking Uncertainty

As time passes and Abby grows into a healthy, active, bright, and happy little girl with just a few more doctor appointments than other kids, my uncertainty is shriveling. It shrinks with each neurology visit until there are no more neurology visits, with each neurosurgical visit, with each subsequent MRI, with each new week in which I am able to speak with physical therapy experts who test weekly and analyze biannually for delays. What is left is the "fine-tuning" of fine and gross motor skills, they tell me, which may even have nothing to do with the original injury.

Similarly, medicine's uncertain future is shrinking as innovations explode alongside technology. In the last 150 years alone, medicine has evolved exponentially. Since groundbreaking changes from the first use of anesthesia in 1846 to the discovery of penicillin in 1928, to vaccines for polio in 1955, to the first laparoscopic surgery in 1981, to the mapping of the human genome in 2003, we know more and more about how to treat medical ailments, giving patients fewer concerns over their ability to heal and live. Or, I should say, at least the medical ailments we know exist.

The Kaplan-Meier estimator, for example, is but one commonly used example of a projected estimation that has served to limit the unknown in prognoses for patients suffering from terminal illnesses. Developed in the mid-1950s by physicians Edward Kaplan and Paul Meier, the Kaplan-Meier estimator is a metric that predicts the probability of survival from a medical condition. When people want to know how much time they have left after a diagnosis of a disease like cancer or the likelihood of a specific treatment working in their favor, physicians often rely on this survival analysis, particularly in the fields of oncology and infectious disease. Anything, even a statistic, that can minimize some of the unknown elements of medicine is revolutionary to how patients and physicians can cope with the inevitable. It coats the process like a cherry flavor in children's cough syrup. It doesn't change the reality of the situation, but perhaps may make taking that medicine more manageable.

Biotechnology is changing so much of this far beyond mere estimates of probability. A relatively new but growing field of medicine that shrinks this uncertainty even more is that of regenerative medicine, focusing specifically on growing new human cells, tissues, and organs through 3D-printing technology. Though still in development, regenerative medicine addresses the reality that there is a tremendous need for organs that is unmatched by their

availability. Some diseases can be overcome with an organ transplant, such as a kidney or a liver or a heart; however, there are far
fewer available transplants for donation than for people waiting on
a transplant list. The result is that many people die waiting for
kidney transplants, lung transplants, heart transplants, bone mar-
row transplants. Their survival, of course, is not certain with a
transplant, but their death is much more certain without one.

In his well-known TED talk, Dr. Anthony Atala, the director
of the Wake Forest Institute for Regenerative Medicine and the
W. Boyce Professor and Chair of Urology at Wake Forest University, said that since 2005, the number of patients requiring an organ has doubled, while in the same time, the actual number of
transplants has barely gone up, leading to a public health crisis. He
has been working for years on developing a 3D-printed kidney.
This process, which began by replacing ink with stem cells in an
inkjet printer years ago, has evolved into a process that may change
organ transplantation and regenerative medicine in the future.
Though these complicated synthetic organs are not yet ready for
human use, the concept is revolutionary. It takes a patient's own
cells into use to print not only the new organ, but an organ that is
likely more suited to be accepted by the body because it is using the
patient's own cells. And if the synthetic organs such as kidneys are
one day viable, it may serve to eliminate some of the uncertainty of
questioning: When will I get off the transplant list? How long
must I wait when I know that the only way I can survive is with
this transplant? How well will my body accept this organ?

Perhaps most tailored to the patient is the concept of personalized healthcare, which may be key in helping to minimize some of the trial and error of medicine. Personalized healthcare, in many ways, is the future of medicine, as it enables doctors to test the patient's genetics, stem cells, and other individualized codes with existing and developing treatments to determine which may be the best fit. In other words, doctors are able to take personal information from patients and test it against drugs to determine a likely outcome. It reduces the risk of trying a treatment that will not work and helps predict which treatment will work for the patient. Though certainly not determinative of survival, this approach may provide the best estimates physicians have at this time to match treatment with illness, returning to Hippocrates's immortal words: "It is more important to know what sort of person has a disease than to know what sort of disease a person has." Or, *treat the patient, not the paper.* This is, in fact, treating the patient far beyond the paper. This is potentially saving months and even years of a cancer patient's quality of life and life expectancy by not wasting time and physical wear by trying a certain radiation or chemotherapy, because doctors know it just won't work on this body or this type of cancer in this person. This is not curing cancer or heart or kidney disease by eliminating it, but it is decreasing some of the vast unknowns that accompany the treatment.

That these innovations are but the beginning of an evolution in medicine does not eradicate the great chasm of the unknown. The Kaplan-Meier scale doesn't take away the disease or tell you how you became sick; it merely predicts your likelihood of survival. The advent of the 3D-printed kidney cannot unequivocally determine that the body will accept the organ, but it does eliminate some of the question of whether a patient will actually have the chance to receive a kidney and improves the chance that the body will accept it if generated from the patient's own cells. In vitro fertilization can enable pregnancy for many women—but not all—and cannot ensure a successful full-term pregnancy. When people presume innovation and expectation, it is not absolute. Absolution is impossible, inside medicine or out.

Neuroplasticity

My father was diagnosed with diabetes in his early seventies, just days before Abby got sick. I remember him telling me with acceptance, matter-of-factly, "I'm just going to work on a new diet and take it from there. My own father had diabetes, so this isn't terribly surprising. I'm seventy-two. The reality is that it is a shorter period of my life I need to worry about diet and death," he said, trying to lighten the mood.

He was only sort of joking, I know, but it made sense. Better at his age to get a disease like diabetes, in which so much of the concern is the long-term damage it will do to your body, how it may affect your longevity, than taking on that diagnosis in his youth. The inverse is true for a stroke in an infant. All things being equal, if it is going to happen, it might be preferable earlier on in a life, while the brain is still forming and neuroplasticity is strong, so there's less of a loss—or perhaps even none at all. No need to relearn how to walk, talk, tell a joke. Those neural connections have not yet been fully made, so they can be rewired before the engine starts.

Neuroplasticity is a wonder, particularly in infancy. Abby's brain, as I would hear during her time in the hospital, is young and immature, not yet developed, and mostly *plastic*. Malleable and interchangeable, it can be rewired, stopped, and started in thousands of ways. Rewiring is merely a small part of our anatomical genius. Redundancy is another. I learned that we have so much brain tissue, particularly in the frontal lobe, that we can live and thrive without a substantial part of it—due to, for example, displacement by a cyst on a Johns Hopkins's valedictorian or a successful rheumatologist.

Neuroplasticity comes from the Greek word *plastikos*, which means "to form." Neuroplasticity, specifically, is the brain's extraordinary ability to reorganize and create new pathways throughout life. When the old passageways are no longer working, the brain can find new paths to travel to do its job and can change its own structure following activity and experience. It does this through repetition and practice, and is most successful early in life before the brain has been set in place. The adage "use it or lose it" is frequent among therapists, both physical and psychological, and is common knowledge among adults. But it is in the early years, specifically from birth until three, that the brain is most plastic. In those early years, the brain is forming and continues until the age of twenty-five, by many new standards. Very few pathways have been made at birth, and by six weeks, very few have been learned. Even more, the anatomy is not complete as the process of myelination—the coating of the neuron, a protection of the nerve cells that helps them conduct signals better—is ongoing in the first few years. By age three, a child's brain has already reached 82 percent of its size, and by age five, it will have grown to 90 percent of its adult size. While doctors hadn't yet discovered this progress of growth in the year 1800, Jean Itard realized himself that he was too late with Victor, the wild boy of Aveyron. Among so many other sources of trauma, he was too late to intervene in Victor's language development. It is in those early years that the plastic brain rewires, making it clear that *some* brain injuries are not necessarily catastrophic at such an early age. They may even become insignificant over time.

A hemispherectomy, for example, can leave a four-year-old paralyzed the morning after surgery, and a few years later, despite a limp, dancing in a ballet recital.

A little boy with a particularly complicated AVM, who bled during brain surgery into the vision control of his brain, can regain his sight, whereas someone double or triple his age would be blind.

A young child raised in three languages can become trilingual by the age of twelve, whereas it would take her parents a lifetime to master all three.

A stroke in a newborn can leave few to no lasting delays.

. . .

BETWEEN WORK AND LIFE, THERE is the continuation of physical therapy, occupational therapy, more early intervention for Abby. I see her brain develop rapidly.

In time, she rolls over.

In time, she crawls.

In time, she turns pages in books and falls in love with them. She even says her first word apart from "Mama."

Book.

She laughs and eats solid foods and selects her own books to read.

She speaks with the diction of a stage actor.

At one, she sings "Edelweiss" from *The Sound of Music* and "Maybe" from *Annie.* She is falling into my indoctrination of the love of musical theater. I come home one day to find her acting out *Newsies* with her babysitter, putting up her fist in the air, singing out, "Seize the day!" She is eighteen months. She knows the musical better than I do.

In time, she walks and runs and jumps and falls in love with trampolines and slides and swings and everything else that children fall in love with. She speaks early, advancing quickly in the verbal and cognitive areas over the slower physical ones, perhaps due to the area of the bleed. Or perhaps that is just her general constitution. We cannot know. She speaks with me in sentences at eighteen months. She communicates fully by two years of age.

I speak to her physical and occupational therapists who consistently tell me that even if delayed, she eventually meets all of their goals in appropriate time and will not need them beyond the first three years.

In a short period of time, Abby has been able to rewire her brain to compensate for the injury. Because of the timing of the insult, she did not need to relearn how to walk, relearn how to talk, how to eat, how to see. She was a blank slate, neurologically. Fully formed and yet not formed at all. From the moment of discharge from the hospital, I know that because of neuroplasticity, rewiring can happen subject to many "ifs." *If* the bleeding stopped *and* would not recur *and* she did not develop hydrocephalus *and* would not need brain surgery, her plastic brain would find new pathways to life. The interstate to normalcy is more difficult to travel, but it is navigable.

Another reason that Google needs a bouncer and statistics need preambles.

At a new neurologist visit, the doctor examines Abby and looks at us in shock. As we did with neurosurgeons, we visit two neurologists to weigh each opinion against the other, even if the same.

"She had a *fourth-degree* bleed?"

Yes, we say, owning the history, along with her recovery and rehabilitation.

"Nobody would know."

We nod.

We know.

I understand the concept, but still want that prognosis. I want to know about long-term effects. I want to know what her life looks like at ten, at fifteen, at twenty-five. What my life looks like at the same projected relative age. What the possibility of having a second child may look like sooner.

I ask every doctor this question and they all respond with the same shrugged shoulders.

What about long-term for all of us?

"There aren't a lot of statistics with an unexplained brain bleed on a six-week-old because it doesn't happen often," the neurologist tells us. "But Abby is doing great. She's thriving. Six weeks seems to be the sweet spot here." She was old enough to begin early intervention right away, but not too old that she'd learned anything already. This doctor, like all the ones before her, gives no prognosis.

We don't need to see this doctor for an entire year.

Improvising

I attend an improv comedy class at the famed Upright Citizens Brigade in Los Angeles. I'm not entirely sure that I do so for the right reasons. I've always wanted to take an improv class and put myself back on the stage where I spent much of my childhood, dreaming of Broadway. I also want to meet new people, challenge myself, and seek humor and comedy where so much of the recent year has drowned in the other half of the dramatic mask. At thirty-six, I think I might be the oldest person in the class. Most students are aspiring actors. Some of them boast years of experience and comfort on stage. Others, like me, are doing it for fun.

We play one game in which each person must stand in the center and become "The Expert." The expert at anything, be it Elmer's Glue or the Theory of Relativity. The rest of us must ask questions, and the expert must answer with anything he or she desires, and we must believe this to be true. In an outside life, I would force the disagreement, require questions. But there is something freeing about asking questions and accepting a new truth. It's not denying the need to question authority or accept blind facts. But, rather, if you know something new is true—if, as the rules of "the expert" game are given, we are supposed to accept this expert's words as true—then we must work within that framework. For the time being.

Only a few rules apply. You must accept the facts you are given and play along. Use the "top of your intelligence," meaning play into the scene given the natural facts you already know, and everything else you don't know, just make up. The same rules applied to the bar exam. When provided with a prompt for which you don't have the answers, create your own framework—your own laws—and answer accordingly within the legal paradigm you've established. The same is true here. You are put on the spot, you are uncomfortable, and you must make do. Interact with others accordingly and accept the sequence of events as either expert or questioner, lawmaker or follower. You are constantly shifting between those roles and they may never find permanence, so you might as well play, live, and . . . go.

Statistical Downfall

I return to the statistics that fueled me with panic for months, filling my imagination with images of different lives altogether. But the statistics have not materialized with Abby. Amir did not suspect they would because of her young age, but his lackluster fear did not change the fact that I relied on those statistics. They provided me with a cursory understanding of what was happening, to help me as I tried to plan disparate versions of our future.

True, sometimes statistics can help, but often they are clumps of facts that do more harm than good. For example, the statistics connected with a Grade IV bleed do not differentiate between three vital factors in our case. First, they do not differentiate between adults and children, or between children and infants. Second, they do not differentiate between the location of the bleed and which part of the brain was compromised. Whether it was a large and redundant lobe, in which very little of the brain is ever actually used, or other more essential parts. Third, they do not necessarily control for the *size* of the actual bleed, despite the defined four distinct gradations. Though a diagnosis of a fourth degree works against her, Abby is fortunate in that all three of these subfactors are in her favor.

Neurological, cognitive, physical, and sensory problems affiliated with this type of a bleed may result, but they may also not result, and it is the latter clause that is often lost in our statistics-needy world while we wait for life to happen. Statistics, which can be nothing more than coffins of numerical parameters, are not human. They are not people; they are papers, numbers, graphs. They are not absolutes. In fact, they are not even given as absolutes, but rather as probabilities, guesses, based on history and other cases—but not necessarily your own. No doctor can provide a precise prognosis of a future for any of us. It would not only be impossible, but also unethical. Doctors treat what is before them. Patients cope with what they are actively experiencing. Neither is a time traveler.

Endlessness

One afternoon, we are driving in the car and Amir pulls over to the side of the road to take a photo of Abby's smile, fearing it is lopsided. He knows that damage from a stroke does not necessarily progress. It is locked in that time and that time is now well in the past. But not in his mind.

Another time, when I am visiting my parents in Dallas with Abby, my mother inadvertently kisses her on the forehead with the remnants of a cold sore on her lips. I find myself petrified in a Dallas ER, illogically begging the physician for prophylactic antivirals *just in case.*

He stares at me, dumbfounded.

"The chances of brain inflammation are so slim. And we'd need to wait days to see if anything even developed."

But I tell him the chances of this bleed were equally slim if not less so, so just prescribe them for her. Please.

Yet another time, Abby has a fever and we question its source, spilling open textbooks in deep sweats only to realize that she was in a ball pit at a children's playroom a day earlier.

Even physicians fall prey to this, despite logic and experience. While out of town, I get a call from Amir who says that Abby has been diagnosed with a rare disease with known cardiac complications. Her temperature spikes and a rash sprouts on nearly every inch of her body. A substitute pediatrician had diagnosed her with Kawasaki's disease, a condition that can cause inflammation in the walls of the arteries, including the heart. Upon hearing this word, Amir immediately walks out of his office and cancels patients for the next few days while Abby undergoes an echocardiogram to rule out the disease. Meanwhile, I hop on the first plane home. By the time I arrive, the rash is gone and the echocardiogram is complete. Abby is holding a red Smurf-like stuffed animal in the shape of a heart, a toy they give out at the pediatric cardiologist's office.

Amir turns to me, exhausted, relieved. He had spent the previous night in the ER at Children's Hospital, unable to wait until the following morning for the echocardiogram. It was almost exactly two years to the date we spent in the same ER with different outcomes. This time, he waited with her eight hours until they were called back and sent away within moments of examination. He told me he flinched when he heard "Neurosurgery" paged overhead.

We had both panicked when we heard the word "Kawasaki's." It didn't take me googling the word to feel the tremor re-enter my body. Another familiar zebra. The same rare condition Amir himself floated to the NICCU team when trying to figure out a cause for the bleed and persistent NICCU fever two years earlier when hoping to find the source of it. Within twenty-four hours of the false diagnosis, no doctor believes she has Kawasaki's. Not her regular pediatrician, not an ER physician, not the cardiologist, and not Amir. A momentary scare evoking memories of the past.

All of this is illogical, though, and I accept it as part of being human, of being a parent, of being a patient. It is paranoia fueled by experience, by the Internet, by a long future spilling out in front of us without a map, but that sliver of doubt—that erosion in complete faith in medicine—is fully present. As it is for Amir. And my sister, and every doctor in my presence. It is perhaps the hidden challenge that propels physicians into the practice of medicine. No doubt the young pediatrician may think twice about sending a newborn for a CT scan following a presentation of vomiting. No doubt we will request additional testing anytime something looks even moderately aberrant. No doubt all doctors have a case early in their careers that embodies this reality. The same is true in every field, every career.

The uncertainty may not have ever entered Abby's mind because it will have resolved before the formation of memory. Abby may have begun the healing process with extraordinary success, but Amir and I now live in constant evolution, revolution, continuation.

And so on we go, heart first into the global and uniformly accepted religion of anxiety that is part of the parenthood badge. It doesn't change, whether you enter at birth, six weeks, or any point thereafter. The concern will always be there. What parent doesn't awaken midsleep, sweaty and fearful that something has happened to his child? What parent doesn't stare feverishly at the monitor, hoping that her child's chest is rising and falling in appropriate meters of breath? If you knew your child could die young, you wouldn't reject parenthood. Amir and I have simply experienced the exquisite fear that defines it a bit early. Abby has already taken the first step for us, providing us with the tools we'll need to parent with an extra hand. Our barometer is now set so high that we don't know what the new pressure point is. When she's eight years old and wants to stay home because of a bitter stomach bug, we'll probably laugh. If she calls from college with a broken leg, we'll tell her to eat some chocolate and buy good crutches. The uncertainty that trails me now is just a part of me. It is there, like my breathing, like my poor eyesight. I put on my contact lenses and continue my day like every other parent, hoping that she continues to do well and follows this upward trajectory—within her health and outside of it.

At two years old, Abby starts preschool. Amir and I tell her teachers about her medical history. Nobody is particularly concerned or shocked, despite the narrative that precedes it. Perhaps this is because they've seen so many derivations in other children or perhaps because Amir and I are sitting with her in an office and it is clear that Abby is no longer the sick baby she was two years earlier. The school administrator looks at us without emotion as if this is nothing. But we need her to know about it just in case.

When we leave on the first day, Abby cries like every other toddler being dropped off at school. Within a week or two, she is excited to go back every morning to see her new friends and teachers. She runs to me when I pick her up, and I embrace her, kissing her cheeks, her nose, her forehead. My fingers brush through her long curly hair, sometimes getting stuck in unruly curls.

We walk home and get ready for the night. Amir completes her evening routine, and just before bed, I walk into the room to kiss her good-night, touching her head to feel for a fontanelle that is no longer there. For now and into the foreseeable future, I still massage that little square inch that rests on top of her like an invisible window. I'll do it when nobody else is looking. I'll do it when not thinking of anything else. My fingers return to the site because it's my form of remembering. I know there is no more soft spot in the skull. I know it has closed beautifully, just barely circumventing a hydrocephalic need for a brain shunt, but I don't know when I'll stop.

The Heisenberg Uncertainty Principle

In the mid-1920s, a young student of theoretical physics arrived in Munich to study under some of the great minds that were working in Germany between the two world wars. Ambitious and innovative, Werner Heisenberg was eager to become a thread in the scientific canvas of that revolutionary time. In the early twentieth century, the world was displaced, and not just militarily and industrially. There was a seismic philosophical shift similarly in the tiny intellectual community of theoretical physicists from the previously held belief in determinism (that the world was predetermined and preordained) to that of quantum mechanics. In 1927, while still under the age of thirty, Heisenberg published what has come to be known as the Uncertainty Principle, changing not only the way scientists approach theoretical physics but also how science is connected to everything else in the world.

In short, the Uncertainty Principle proclaims that it is impossible to know the exact position and the exact momentum of a certain particle at one point in time. To measure a subatomic particle, we utilize light. The light itself will interact with the particle, thereby changing the particle's trajectory (its position and/or momentum), making it impossible to measure both attributes of the particle simultaneously. In other words, the act of observing something changes it. In even other words, there is a natural limit to how much we can know, to how precise our measurements are. Things exist within a cloud of probability.

THE TINCTURE OF TIME

For those of us who panic whenever physics, quantum or otherwise, enters the conversation, it is as basic as saying that we need to breathe to live. A scientifically complex theory in the abstract, but in reality, a concept so straightforward that it has been attributed to almost every field that can be studied. Though nothing more than a study of theories and probabilities, it has achieved, as writer-physicist David Lindley writes in his book *Uncertainty: Einstein, Heisenberg, Bohr, and the Struggle for the Soul of Science,* "a remarkable level of intellectual celebrity." Its omnipresence has made it commonplace.

This discovery established a precedent of, well, of pure unknowingness, which, yielded from field to field, has been taken in as its own orphan of intelligentsia in nearly every creative discipline. Artists and academics and writers and philosophers invoke its name as they attempt to make sense of their worlds. As of the writing of this book, the Library of Congress lists 4,570 books as dealing with "uncertainty," and more specifically, 45 with Heisenberg's Uncertainty Principle alone. It is referenced both correctly and incorrectly in television and the movies, novels and essays, and this is its legacy, for better or for worse. Heisenberg captured a truth that is neither scientific nor unscientific, but merely truth. I'll leave the discussion of its details to the scientific experts, but Heisenberg's legacy bears liturgy. Nearly a century ago, Heisenberg, at the initial refuse of intellectual giants like Albert Einstein, attempted to drop a question mark into a previously held sea of periods. Nothing is ever fully known, he divulged, whether intentionally or otherwise, even in science. Especially in science.

A small article by Dr. Amnon Sonnenberg in the *American Journal of Gastroenterology* titled "A Medical Uncertainty Principle" approaches healthcare within Heisenberg's paradigm. "By analogy," he writes:

> Obviously, a balance needs to be found between pursuing a diagnosis through an extensive workup and compromising the patient's health through this process. . . . [Forcing us] to ask ourselves whether we really need perfect knowledge or whether we could make sound medical decisions given a "calculated" amount of uncertainty. The answer is perhaps in the final thoughts. We can calculate the amount of uncertainty as best as we can, while waiting for the outcome.

Theorems don't matter, though, when you are staring at a heart-rate monitor and hearing the *beep-beep-beep* as you measure it against the ticking of the clock. Relativity, references, cats in boxes, and disagreements among dead German physicists are pointless when you are in a waiting room desperate to hold your child, fantasizing about kissing her and taking her home, aching to push away the irascible questions of whether you'll be suddenly childless, or changing the diapers of a twenty-one-year-old, or at your child's college graduation. Uncertainty principles apply to life, but they are more than numbers, particularly when they clearly require an acceptance of powerlessness. Because that's what it is. A sense of unknowingness, realizing that you can't have all the answers and neither can your doctors, the people who rely on facts, who rely on knowing information.

If I can't know everything about a medical scenario at a given time, I must accept the facts that I do know at that time, acknowledging that they are only part of the complete picture. The human body is so exquisitely rife with question marks that accepting this reality may be one of the few bits of knowledge we can cling to. But this is my story, and it is true of *this* medicine at *this* point in time. It is true of the autism spectrum, of monoclonal gammopathy of undetermined significance, of unexplained infertility, of the speed and origin of so many cancers, of undifferentiated connective tissue diseases, and of so much more. We don't always know why people get cancer, but we know how to treat many forms of it. We don't know what autism is exactly, but we are working on addressing its symptoms, its source, and always on finding a cure. It is very difficult to find a cure for something, though, that is not fully known. So on we research, on we hope, on we go.

What remains as a little irritant occupying our headspace is that science, we know, is based in fact. It is supposed to be an exception to all of this. In science and medicine, there is generally a hypothesis, which is tested and proved or disproved. This is the nature of the more objective fields of study—of hard sciences, of mathematics, of hypotheses with provable theorems. And yet, still, if this hard-proved world that is knowingly governed by facts is *required* to accept uncertainty as fact, then the outside civilian world—the world of faith and creativity and emotions and subjectivity—must also accept uncertainty as fact. As Lindley says, "Therein lies the metaphorical appeal of Heisenberg's uncertainty principle. It doesn't make journalism or anthropology or literary criticism scientific. Rather, it tells us that scientific knowledge, like our general, informal, understanding of the everyday world we inhabit, can be both rational and accidental, purposeful and contingent. Scientific truth is powerful, but not all-powerful."

So, too, is medicine, in its truth. Powerful in its depth, in its ability to perform brain surgery in utero, to map out the human genome, to temporarily stall the heart to exchange it with a better one, though it cannot look into the future and tell us how a pregnancy will develop, how children will grow, if our bodies will fall in line with our parents' courses of health, if genetic predispositions will be inherited, if our eyes will stay lucid, if our skin will remain smooth, if our hair will lose its pigment.

A psychologist I meet with in Los Angeles tells me that "life is about creating fictions." Getting a diagnosis, known or otherwise, requires the same approach. "How do we create a narrative that will sustain us through the exile of uncertainty? Through the exile of the medical unknown?" he says. "As long as there is life, as long as we know that we are not waiting to die, there is something to do." And even if we are waiting to die, there may still be something to do in those final days.

From the moment Abby is hospitalized, I begin this process unknowingly. I am writing internally. I am rewriting. I am revising always. I have spent my life writing stories preparing for this moment. I am living in a narrative I create and continue to rewrite on the page and off. And so will Abby.

Others focus on a sense of control. Amir spends all his time researching neurosurgery and neurology and zebras in newborns to try to find an answer. And he continues to look at life through his trained diagnostic eyes with skepticism, knowing how malleable medicine is, how precarious and fragile it is, how it evolves daily.

Like the wallpapered doilies of blood.

Like framed crystals of gout.

I met with a young father whom I came to know following his series of articles on the *Huffington Post* and videos on YouTube, in which he speaks about his daughter, who was diagnosed with a rare degenerative neurological disorder called RETT syndrome. Online he posts video journals of their life. In person, he hosts a comedy fundraiser every few months to raise awareness and money for research for RETT syndrome. Creative control. Doing everything he can within his power to help others, and in turn himself, to fill in that gap of the unknown.

Others show their gratitude for the outcome by trying to give back. My friend Kendall began doing pro bono work for cancer research centers and even shaved her head to raise money and awareness for research for St. Baldrick's Foundation for childhood cancers.

Sophie and so many others rely on their faith, frequenting church or synagogue or mosque to request prayers and help, never relinquishing the one thing that provides them with answers, comfort, solace, and strength. Faith. The belief that a higher power—whatever it is to you—has the answers, freeing you from much of the anxious pain that you may otherwise experience.

Others find distinct ways to rewrite their narrative, like my friend Adam in creating and establishing his gym and preparing his family financially and personally for what is to come. Or another friend, an active skier, hiker, and runner, who elected to amputate his foot after a devastating canyoneering accident left it permanently injured, all in order to have greater control over his future activity and mobility.

All of it is an illusion of some sort. We never truly know what may come next, but the control, the creativity, the faith, helps us as we navigate the present and the future without a complete picture, a complete answer. We cannot know the position and the momentum at the same time.

I rely on perhaps a combination of faith, control, and creativity. My faith in medicine is still present, though I'm now accepting of its holes and even primed to anticipate them. When doctors tell me there are only slight percentage chances of something going wrong in anything at all, be it my own health, Amir's, or Abby's, I now focus perhaps longer than I should on those outlying percentages—on those zebras. Zebras are not unicorns, after all. I try to control my surroundings as best I can without losing semblance of self, without stopping life, without changing behavior to a point of invisibility. And I create a narrative that evolves daily.

"Scientific truth is powerful, but not all-powerful."

And it is these words upon which we rely in approaching the uncertainties in our health. Heisenberg was twenty-six when he made this discovery. I am thirty-six when I try to understand it beyond its intellectual celebrity.

I am still trying.

Follow-ups

Our two-year neurology follow-up is on a beautiful blue day in Los Angeles, not too dissimilar from that sunny day in March. Amir and I once again pile into the car to drive across town to see the doctor who will hopefully write down on paper what we already know. So far, all of our suspicions, our open and positive projected forecasts lie in our minds, in the minds of physical and occupational therapists, in the trained instincts of her doctors. They are presumptions based on gut, research, intelligence, experience. But they are not on paper. I want the paper trail of clarity, or as much clarity as I can have.

Amir and Abby and I walk into the office and wait together. My hair is still short, but now it is washed and this time healthy. Abby's is long—as long as a four-year-old's hair—and pulled back into a ponytail. Amir and Abby are playing a music game. For more than two years, our musical tastes have been divided. I've introduced show tunes and classical music, and Amir has pretty much introduced everything else. Within one or two beats of hearing a song, Abby can identify the musician.

We are called back to the neurologist's office, where we wait for her to make her long-awaited assessment. It is doubtful that a musical memory that could win her free tickets on a radio game show could serve as that documentation I want of neuro-plasticity.

The neurologist asks Abby to snap her fingers, run down the hall, draw pictures, interact. She flexes her ankles. She spends no more than ten, fifteen minutes with us, and Abby passes all her tests. The neurologist writes something down. She tells us we don't need to come back. We are discharged. There doesn't appear to be anything more to worry about at this time.

Abby has no idea why my heart is released. To her, this is just another doctor's visit. She's grown comfortable with them, excited to see her favorite pediatrician, yet shirking in fear like a toddler when she sees a nurse with a possible needle. But I look to Amir, even more relieved than I was when the neurosurgeon told us we had graduated from neurosurgery.

Amir's relief is less obvious, though.

"I guess I didn't need to see it on paper, because I see her every day," he says.

The documentation didn't matter because medical reality is what governs for him.

For me, though, it is both life and its documentation that reigns.

Documentation

Our childhood memories have a way of reshaping life for us. In my memory, the New Orleans operating room was as large as an airport. When I was in another operating room twenty-five years later, giving birth, I marveled at the radically different sensory experience—small, cold, impersonal, the opposite of my long-standing memorialized fantasy. Was I reinventing life for the purposes of adulthood or had my perspective merely shifted?

Sometimes I flip through the photos on my iPhone and come across the videos from that night, frame-by-frame memorials for the hours between the two emergency room visits. Notes reside, too; emotions I transcribed onto my computer every night. When it seems like so much time has passed that I can't possibly remember those days, I open up the document and read. Or I flip through the photos on my phone, or I scavenge all of the paperwork and signage, visitors' stickers and jewelry. The armband Abby is assigned when admitted to each ER, each CT, each MRI, is also taped around my wrist in larger, identical form. The name the same, the identity the same on paper. I have filled a drawer with them.

These armbands, bracelets really, tell their own story, as do the photos and videos. Like staring into a puddle, they are warped reflections of what happened and what continues to happen, of reality and my perspective of reality. Two white hospital bands—one tiny and one full-sized—means something similar to anyone who sees them. A photograph of an infant flanked with tubes and wires does, too. Videos, although open to slightly different interpretation, are perhaps the best evidence of what's occurring physically. But emotions can be trickier to document. They are the intangibles, the unseen evidence of trauma, and they all reside in, as Eli Wiesel says, our own "kingdom of memory."

A mosaic of memories comes together in this drawer, on my hard drive, in my mind, when I struggle to tell this story. For every sticker, every parking receipt, every Get Well Soon card, there is something invisible that accompanies it. Words. Often as inaccurate as even medical records—which can document events wrong, misdiagnose, write names incorrectly, and overall question the history of an incident altogether—words tell a story from a certain perspective. And the words that flowed onto my screen while beside Abby's incubator follow me like all of the video evidence follows her.

But still, video is unquestionably accurate. Images are supposed to be true. Particularly when looking at them evolve over a year's worth of time. Two years. Ten. A lifetime. Which documentation will be the most authentic? The drawer of artifacts or this book? Or neither. They both reside in neighboring states in my own kingdom.

Daniel Kahneman argues that everything we do is *for* our memories. We are slaves to the remembering parts of our selves. Though Kahneman defines different types of memory in his

work, he is actually suggesting a distinction in terms of determining happiness between experience and memory, in the space
between "being happy in your life versus being happy *about* your
life." He calls these two memories the "experiencing memory"
and the "remembering memory." And he concludes that psychological memory, or the experience of the moment, lasts only
about three seconds.

Three seconds?

If this is true, then you've already forgotten the experience of
reading most of this chapter, let alone the entire book that precedes it. Perhaps by the end of this book, you are happy, which
makes this reading experience positive. Or the inverse. Because
Abby has narrowly escaped a statistic, the book ends with joy, but
does it take away any of the emotions experienced while reading
it? Had the statistics been realized, would it not be happy merely
because it would be a different normal? Certainly not, as we
would embrace whatever reality would be given to us. But my
kingdom of memory is now a mixture of happiness and sadness,
joy and fear, anxiety and acceptance. Retrospectively, most
things can be and in many ways are.

During her hospitalization, Amir and I said to each other so
much, *Thank goodness she won't remember this.* Not the pain. Not
the fear. Not the visuals. But so much of life is needing to remember. Capturing the pain, securing those memories, just like the
blood caught in the plastic tape wrapped around her arm to
secure her IV. Seeing it confirmed what I knew to be true.

One Plus One

Abby is healthy enough now that I am ready to give her a sibling. This second time does not take quite as long to conceive. Seven years of one attempt shrunk into a handful of months for another, and after four months of trying, I casually tell Amir that I am pregnant again while just sitting in bed. We take a video of a twenty-month Abby at Halloween, shortly after we learn our news. She is wearing purple scrubs and dressed as a doctor. She wears a yellow stethoscope, which she knows how to use and pronounce. We want to announce our news to our family, so we try to get her to say, "A baby!" when asked, "What's in Mommy's belly?" She pulls out the stethoscope, and when Amir asks the question, she cries out, "It's a *new* baby!"

I cannot know how I'll feel when I bring home a second child until I do. I am nervous about travel and consumption and ultra-sounds, but there is nothing I can do apart from keeping my body safe and healthy. I must wait the nine months. I must go home and enjoy the next child when I am able. I must bear with nerves through the twenty-week ultrasound when an OB will spot prob-lems or not. The memories will return with each new visit. Early in the pregnancy, I undergo diagnostic testing, as I did with Abby in the form of a CVS—chorionic villus sampling—a close cousin of the amniocentesis. I welcome it because while invasive and heavy with potential risk of miscarriage, it will eliminate some of the uncertainty of pregnancy. It will provide me with as much knowledge that can be ascertained ahead of time regarding possible genetic disorders. I want to know that information. I wanted to know it with Abby, too.

The CVS comes and goes, and we learn that there are no genetic abnormalities that are testable. Still, I go in for ultrasound after ultrasound, eliminating a bit more (but not all) of the unknowns of the baby's development. I am nervous about this pregnancy, but no more so than any person is nervous about a developing body inside of her. I can't question the past. I cannot look to my first pregnancy and first child to determine the health of the second. Questioning the past is a practice as futile as running on a treadmill to cross a bridge. You'll never go anywhere. The only thing to do is get off the treadmill and walk across the bridge.

The Future

I stare at a photograph of Abby on the emergency gurney at Children's Hospital and the flood of those memories rushes back to me. I am sure that I'll stare at it in ten years or in thirty, when this is nothing but a personal mythology. In it, eight hands and feet flank her diminutive torso. Her two hands, her two feet, exposed and handcuffed with labels and gauze, tape and splints. Blue plastic gloves cover four more hands, the medical personnel expertly holding her down. My exposed hand holds a light blue pacifier to her mouth, plugging it, providing an attempt at calmness, though I was anything but calm. Six thick wires are taped to her chest.

Four metallic stickers pasted anywhere there is space to account for her heartbeat, her breathing, her pulse. Band-Aids taped erratically on various open spaces garnish the final opening.

I count eight limbs attached to her—some from myself, from her own body, from doctors and nurses all reaching out to touch her and heal her. And that's when I see it. She is the Indian goddess Durga, one of the most powerful deities in Hinduism, the fierce warrior, alive and powerful with eight or more arms; she has battled evil—in her case, injury—and emerged triumphantly. Abby is not the sick infant, nor the lively and intelligent toddler. She is a reclaimed narrative to be anything at all. A beautifully uncertain future as a teacher, an artist, a doctor or a nurse, a parent or an aunt, a friend, a partner, a student, a business person, a politician, a musician, an innovator, a dreamer, a creator, a builder, a worker, a leader, a follower, an athlete, a scholar, a writer, a sister, a daughter. This is now the story that matters. Everything that comes next. And I have no idea what it will be, and this fills me with joy, with anxiety, with love, with passion, and with anticipation. It will be her narrative written from scratch. Not a story of wires tunneling through her barely formed skin or hours in rehabilitation rewiring her chemistry, but that of a symbol, a new narrative. Anything but a princess.

SOMETIMES AMIR AND I SIT on the couch watching Abby play. Most people say that they wouldn't know what happened if they didn't know. Even I look at her and I can't tell. I never want to be that parent who cries from the rooftop with joy when her kid rolls over or walks or talks for the first time.

But we didn't know if we were going to get those, Amir and I say to each other. We might not have gotten them.

I nod my head.

I try not to worry.

The excitement of watching each milestone is all the more profound.

And we both feel gratitude.

Literature and quantum mechanics and behavioral psychology and memory whirl in my head and I think of peace. Abby latching to my breast in her first minutes of life. Her first birthday party. Her first steps. Her first days of preschool.

The ache of not knowing what will come next covers my heart with every bit of what Google once told me it would. On my latest search, I see what the world thinks of uncertainty. Whether it differs or is aligned with my own this time around. Five autofills complete the space.

Uncertainty is the essence of romance.

Uncertainty is certain.

Uncertainty is a virtue.

Uncertainty is the only certainty there is.

Uncertainty is the refuge of hope.

Nowhere in the top five does it say, "Uncertainty is killing me."

And for once, I agree.

Acknowledgments

I am indebted to the following people:

To my brilliant agent, Richard Pine, without whom none of this would have been possible. He believed in this book when I handed him a short essay about the unknown future, and I am forever indebted to him. To my extraordinary editor, Emily Cunningham, who saw what I hoped to do with this book so early and shepherded it into existence. Thank you for pushing my boundaries and working with me with such kindness, intelligence, and respect. To Jonathan Burnham at Harper, where this book was initially born, who generously gave the blessing to allow it to move with Emily to Penguin Press. To the entire team at Penguin Press for believing in this book and putting forth such effort to bring it to the public, especially the president and publisher, Ann Godoff and Scott Moyers. Thank you to the production editor, Tess Espinoza; to the cover designer, Darren Haggar; interior designer, Amanda Dewey; copyeditor, John Jusino; to my publicist,

Juli Kiyan; and Matt Boyd and Grace Fisher, for their hard work in marketing this book to the public.

An avalanche of gratitude goes out to the team of doctors and nurses and therapists who cared for my daughter and helped her recover, rehabilitate, and grow into a thriving, funny, active, confident, and bright girl. To Dr. Nareen Hindoyan, one of the kindest and most generous physicians caring for children today, and to the entire emergency department and NICCU at Children's Hospital Los Angeles. To the Regional Centers in Southern California and to the physical and occupational therapists who visited our home weekly, especially Dr. Cheryl Hubert and Birthe Stern Minnick. A special level of love for the kindhearted babysitters who not only helped us while we worked, but also gave openly with their hearts. To Elizabeth Dalla Betta and Elyse Fulton. You made A's first years warm, comforted, and full of joy.

Thank you to the dozens of people who welcomed a conversation about uncertainty in medicine, and shared their own stories with me. To protect their privacy, I have not written their names in this book, but their words touched me, moved me, and transformed my vision of life.

To experts in the scientific, psychological, and theological worlds, especially Andy Hoffman; Imam Tauquer Shah; Rabbi Ed Feinstein; Ernest Katz, PhD; Avihay Kadosh, PhD; Patricia Krief, MD; Adrienne Hollander, MD; Alan Kaplan, MD; Craig Fox, PhD. Thank you also to Laura Splan; Prakash Venkataraman; Lori Uscher-Pines, PhD; and Audrey Reichman, PhD.

Thank you to several friends who never stop holding my hand. To Jen Nevas, Virginia Talley, Kaylyn Betts, Becky Wasserman, Dina Danon. To early readers and dear writer friends whose thoughts helped me put my own on paper, especially Emma Claire Sweeney, Harriet Levin Millan, Emily Bullock, and Jennifer Pooley. Thank you to the UCROSS Foundation, and Sarah Jagels and the St. Malo Beach House for the generous space and time to write.

Mostly, a book like this could not be written without the love and support of my family, "Abby's" family, who have loved both of us throughout the process of this book and most important, her rehabilitation. Thank you to everyone related to A, who read and reread this book in advance as her advocate. To my mom and dad, Charles and Kathi Silver, whose constant support and love for A and for me are with us daily. Special thanks to my father, a man whose life is a treasure map of inspiration, and who was both brave and generous to open his narrative to me and all who read this book. To my mother-in-law, Etty, who was living a parallel experience of medical uncertainty while I was writing this. To my father-in-law, Mordechai, who I'll always miss, who taught me so much about love and generosity and kindness. To my siblings, Arielle and Sasha, who are my extra limbs, and my nieces Leah and Ilana, who complete A's world. To Yael, who is my catastrophic insurance, and to my nephew, Yossi, who is A's surrogate big brother. And of course, to little L, the newest member of our family, who will change my life in ways I cannot know.

To Amir, with whom life is balanced and peaceful, for whom fatherhood has provided a revived sense of self. For such a private person to be so comfortable with the profound exposure of memoir is formidable. Thank you for supporting everything in this book from its inception, and for not once questioning the components that include you. I love you.

Mostly, for A. This book is for you. Every word in it is infused with my gratitude for your life.

Further Reading

In my search to try and understand uncertainty, I read novels, memoirs, plays, scholarly articles, medical studies, and so much more. This list is inclusive of what I read, though it is not comprehensive of every word. Many of these texts have inspired the book in part, while others served as intellectual foundations. I hope this list of reading materials will be of help to others going through similar experiences.

Memoir

Bialosky, Jill. *History of a Suicide*. New York: Atria, 2011.

Biss, Eula. *On Immunity*. Minneapolis: Graywolf Press, 2014.

Cahalan, Susannah. *Brain on Fire: My Month of Madness*. New York: Free Press, 2012.

Deraniyagala, Sonali. *Wave*. New York: Knopf, 2013.

Didion, Joan. *The Year of Magical Thinking*. New York: Knopf, 2005.

———. *Blue Nights*. New York: Knopf, 2011.

Grealy, Lucy. *Autobiography of a Face*. New York: Houghton Mifflin, 1994.

Karr, Mary. *The Art of Memoir*. New York: Harper, 2015.

FURTHER READING

MacDonald, Helen. *H Is for Hawk*. New York: Grove Atlantic, 2015.

Manguso, Sarah. *The Two Kinds of Decay*. New York: Farrar, Straus and Giroux, 2008.

———. *Ongoingness*. Minneapolis: Graywolf Press, 2015.

Marsh, Henry. *Do No Harm: Stories of Life, Death, and Brain Surgery*. New York: Thomas Dunne Books, 2015.

McCracken, Elizabeth. *An Exact Replica of a Figment of My Imagination*. New York: Little Brown and Company, 2008.

Nelson, Maggie. *The Argonauts*. Minneapolis: Graywolf Press, 2016.

O'Rourke, Meghan. *The Long Goodbye*. New York: Riverhead, 2011.

Patchett, Anne. *Truth & Beauty*. New York: Harper, 2004.

Rapp, Emily. *The Still Point of the Turning World*. New York: Penguin Press, 2013.

Roth, Philip. *The Facts: A Novelist's Autobiography*. New York: Farrar, Straus and Giroux, 1988.

Shapiro, Dani. *Devotion*. New York: Harper, 2010.

Skloot, Rebecca. *The Immortal Life of Henrietta Lacks*. New York: Crown, 2010.

Smith, Claire Bidwell. *The Rules of Inheritance*. New York: Plume, 2012.

Solnit, Rebecca. *A Field Guide to Getting Lost*. New York: Viking, 2005.

———. *The Faraway Nearby*. New York: Viking, 2013.

Strauss, Darin. *Half a Life*. New York: Random House Trade Paperbacks, 2011.

Verghese, Abraham. *My Own Country*. New York: Simon and Schuster, 1994.

Woodward, Theodore E. *Make Room for Sentiment: A Physician's Story*. Baltimore: University of Maryland Alumni, 1988.

GENERAL NONFICTION AND CRITICISM

Albert, David Z. *Quantum Mechanics and Experience*. Cambridge: Harvard University Press, 1993.

Doidge, Norman. *The Brain's Way of Healing: Remarkable Discoveries and Recoveries from the Frontiers of Neuroplasticity*. New York: Viking, 2015.

Fadiman, Anne. *The Spirit Catches You and You Fall Down*. New York: Farrar, Straus and Giroux, 1997.

Fahey, Caitlin Jeanne. "Altogether Governed by Humours: The Four Ancient Temperaments in Shakespeare." Graduate theses and dissertations. http://scholarcommons.usf.edu/etd/230. 2008.

Gawande, Atul. *Complications*. New York: Metropolitan Books, 2002.

———. *Being Mortal*. New York: Metropolitan Books, 2014.

Gordon, Lois. *Reading Godot*. New Haven and London: Yale University Press, 2002.

Kahneman, Daniel. *Thinking Fast and Slow*. New York: Farrar, Straus and Giroux, 2011.

Kluger, Matthew J. *Fever: Its Biology, Evolution, and Function*. Princeton: Princeton University Press, 1979.

Lane, Harlan. *Wild Boy of Aveyron*. Cambridge: Harvard University Press, 1979.

Lindley, David. *Uncertainty: Einstein, Heisenberg, Bohr, and the Struggle for the Soul of Science*. New York: Anchor Books, 2007.

Mukherjee, Siddhartha. *The Emperor of All Maladies*. New York: Scribner, 2010.

Sacks, Oliver. *The Man Who Mistook His Wife for a Hat*. New York: Touchstone, 1998.

———. *Hallucinations*. New York: Knopf, 2012.

Serpeli, Namwali C. *Seven Modes of Uncertainty*. Cambridge: Harvard University Press, 2014.

Shonkoff, Jack P., and Samuel J. Meisels. *Handbook of Early Intervention, Second Edition*. Cambridge, UK: Cambridge University Press, 2000.

Smyth, M. D., J. Charley, et al. *History of Rheumatology in the United States*. Atlanta: Arthritis Foundation, 1985.

Sontag, Susan. *Illness as Metaphor and AIDS and Its Metaphors*. New York: Picador, 2001.

Fiction, Poetry, and Drama

Alexie, Sherman. "Learning to Drown." *Beloit Poetry Journal* 41, no. 1 (1990).

Beckett, Samuel. *Waiting for Godot*. New York: Grove Press, 2011.

Cervantes, Miguel de. *Don Quixote.*

Dawson, Jill. *Wild Boy*. London: Sceptre, 2003.

Dostoevsky, Fyodor. *Crime and Punishment.*

Poe, Edgar Allen. "The Tell-Tale Heart." *The Tell-Tale Heart and Other Writings.* New York: Bantam Classics, 1983.

Shaffer, Peter. *Amadeus.* New York: Harper & Row, 1981.

Shakespeare, William. *Hamlet.*

———. *Macbeth.*

Stoppard, Tom. *Rosencrantz and Guildenstern Are Dead.* New York: Grove Press, 1971.

HISTORICAL TEXTS

Bartlett, Elisha, MD. *Diagnosis and Treatment of the Fevers of the United States.* 4th edition. Philadelphia: Blanchard & Lea, 1856.

Bucknill, John Charles. *The Medical Knowledge of Shakespeare.* London: Longman & Co., Paternoster Row, 1860.

Hippocrates of Kos and Professor Sir Geoffrey Ernest Richard Lloyd. Translated by J. Chadwick, W. N. Mann, I. M. Lonie, et al. *Hippocratic Writings.* New York: Penguin Classics, 1983.

Maimonides, Moses. Translated by M. Fiedlaender; edited and compiled by Paul A. Boer Sr. *A Guide for the Perplexed.* Veritas Splendor Publications, 2013.

Münsterberg, Hugo. *On the Witness Stand: Essays on Psychology and Crime.* Ithaca: Cornell University Library, 2009; originally published in 1908.

Osler, William, MD. *Aequanimitas.* New York: McGraw-Hill, 1905.

ARTICLES, ESSAYS, AND STUDIES

Atkins, E. "Fever: Historical Perspectives and Evolution of Modern Views." *British Journal of Rheumatology* (1985).

Clarke, Sir Cyril. "The Uncertainty Principle as Applied to Medicine." *Journal of Biological Education* 16, no. 2 (1982): 93–96.

"Dr. Anthony Atala, MD: New Body Parts—the Shape of Things to Come?" World Intellectual Property Organization. *WIPO Magazine* (June 2013).

Engelhardt, Laura. "The Problem with Eyewitness Testimony: Commentary on a Talk by George Fisher and Barbara Tversky." *Stanford Journal of Legal Studies* 1, no. 1.

Fox, Craig R., and Russell A. Poldrack. "Prospect Theory and the Brain." *Neuroeconomics: Decision Making and the Brain.* Elsevier (2009).

Hamilton, Jon. "A Man's Incomplete Brain Reveals Cerebellum's Role in Thought and Emotion." NPR.org. March 16, 2015.

Harris, Elizabeth A. "Sharp Rise in Occupational Therapy Cases at New York's Schools." *New York Times.* February 17, 2015.

Johnston, Carol S., and Lori L. Thompson. "Vitamin C Status of an Outpatient Population." *Journal of the American College of Nutrition* 17, no. 4 (1998).

Kaplan, E. L., and P. Meier. "Nonparametric Estimation from Incomplete Observations." *Journal of the American Statistical Association* 53 (1958): 457–81.

Kennerley, Steven W., and Mark E. Walton, et al. "Optimal Decision Making and the Anterior Cingulate Cortex." *Nature Neuroscience* 9, no. 7 (July 2006).

Kottek, Samuel S., MD. "Toward Becoming an Accomplished Physician: Maimonides Versus Galen." *Rambam Maimonides Medical Journal* 2, no. 4 (October 2011).

Mundkur, Nandini. "Neuroplasticity in Children." *Indian Journal of Pediatrics* 72 (October 2005).

Naidoo, T. "Health and Health Care—a Hindu Perspective." *Medicine and Law* 7, no. 6 (1989): 643–47.

Rich, Jason T., and Neely J. Gail, et al. "A Practical Guide to Understanding Kaplan-Meier Curves." *Otolaryngology Head Neck Surgery* 143, no. 3 (September 2010): 331–36.

Sonnenberg, Amnon, MD. "A Medical Uncertainty Principle." Elsevier Science Inc. M.Sc. *American Journal of Gastroenterology* 96, no. 12 (2001).

Wellbery, Caroline. "The Art of Medicine. The Value of Medical Uncertainty." *The Lancet* 375 (May 2010).

Whitman, Sarah M., M.D. "Pain and Suffering as Viewed by the Hindu Religion." *Journal of Pain* 8, no. 8 (August 2007): 607–13.

FURTHER READING

Videos, Lectures, and Interview Transcripts

Aamodt, Sandra. Interview by Tony Cox. "Brain Maturity Extends Well Beyond Teen Years." *National Public Radio: Brain Candy.* October 10, 2011.

Atala, Anthony. "Printing a Human Kidney." TED2011. Filmed March 2011.

BBC Radio 4. *Case Study: The Wild Boy of Aveyron.* May 2008. http://www .bbc.co.uk/programmes/b00b7lrb.

Gottlieb, Michael A., and Rudolf Pfeiffer. "The Relation of Wave and Particle Viewpoints." *The Feynman Lectures on Physics.* California Institute of Technology. http://www.feynmanlectures.caltech.edu/III _02.html.

Kahneman, Daniel. "The Riddle of Experience vs. Memory." TED2010. Filmed February 2010.

Pamphlets

"Funding the Work of California's Regional Centers." Prepared by the Association of Regional Center Agencies. September 2013. http://www .chhs.ca.gov/DSTaskForce/7%20Funding-the-Work-of-CA-RCs -Report.pdf.

"Economic Acting Lessons: Using Insights into Human Behavior, UCLA Anderson Special Research Group Is Helping to Transform Economics." UCLA Anderson School of Business. *Assets;* Fall 2009. http://www .anderson.ucla.edu/assets-archive/fall-2009-x32918#economic.

Reference Books

Diagnostic and Statistical Manual of Mental Disorders, 5th edition. Edited by the American Psychiatric Association. Arlington, VA: American Psychiatric Association Publishing, 2013.

Stedman's Medical Dictionary, 26th edition. Baltimore: Williams & Wilkins, 2005.